Poetry of Presence

An Anthology of Mindfulness Poems

Merry Christmas,
Julia — 2017
Paul & Janet

Poetry of Presence

An Anthology of Mindfulness Poems

Phyllis Cole-Dai & Ruby R. Wilson

Editors

To Julia
May you always be
where you are.
Ruby R. Wilson

GRAYSON BOOKS

WEST HARTFORD, CT

www.GraysonBooks.com

Poetry of Presence: An Anthology of Mindfulness Poems

ISBN: 978-0-9982588-3-6
Published by Grayson Books
West Hartford, Connecticut
Printed in the USA

Library of Congress Control Number: 201793836

Interior & Cover Design: Cindy Mercier
Cover Photo: David Moynahan Photography

GraysonBooks.com

Praise for *Poetry of Presence*

"Reading poetry is *transitional meditation*. Reading great poetry is like finding a breath on the page that's your own. Together these poets form a powerful sea of words. Individually, each poem is a story coming to life. I'll keep this by my side to read one poem a day to return to a state of mindfulness, breathing language through the heart. If you choose one anthology, I say let it be this one for the amazement—for the voices that, surprisingly, will speak to what you want to find in yourself."

—Grace Cavalieri, host and producer, *The Poet and the Poem from the Library of Congress*

"The poems in this book, arranged gently and creatively, are an invitation to mindful presence and to a world where words and phrases initiate us, wake us up, and guide us home."

—Kelly Boys, host of *The Year of Mindfulness* and mindfulness consultant to the United Nations Foundation

"These poems remind us to live 'undefended.' To stand, deliberately and consciously, as witnesses of the present moment. To gaze upon existence from the place of Divine Intimacy. To reach out from that place to those who suffer. Living this way takes lots of practice. *Poetry of Presence* will be a companion and guide, leading us into deeper communion with the world."

—Fr. Richard Rohr, founder of the Center for Action and Contemplation, and author of such books as *The Naked Now: Learning to See as the Mystics See*

"After reading just a poem or two in *Poetry of Presence*, I started quieting down, breathing easier. The poems had already begun to do their work. What a gift! This will be a book I will return to again and again to find the peaceful presence I need to face the day."

—Megan Scribner, co-author of *Teaching with Heart: Poetry that Speaks to the Courage to Teach*

"Especially in times of challenge, I turn to poetry in my life, and in my work. Poetry expresses the ineffable—that which is beyond logic and linear thinking—like God, or love or presence. In my mindfulness teaching, poetry is always present and I look forward to using the poems in this beautiful collection on a regular basis."

—Rabbi Jill Berkson Zimmerman, founder of the Jewish Mindfulness Network

to

the poets who help us be mindful
in a world that has urgent need of presence

Contents

The Invitation

Some poems are good medicine. They soothe our anxieties and self-doubt, restore our balance, boost our energy and strength, help us cope with stress, or even heal. Such poems we tend to keep, and share. We dogear their pages. We copy them down in our journals. We mull them over in times of reflection. We pass them around in book clubs, support groups and classrooms. We send them to loved ones and friends. We read them aloud to mark special days, to observe sacred days, to endure sad days. We utter them like prayers.

Many of these "good medicine" poems are *mindful*. Mindfulness is a buzzword these days, whether in health and wellness, parenting, education, the workforce, counseling, spirituality... but what does it mean? Here's one way to understand it: *Mindfulness is keeping our heads and hearts where our bodies are*. Moment by moment, we sustain a deep, nonjudgmental awareness of our thoughts, emotions, physical sensations and surroundings, right where we are.

In reading this page, for example, you invest your full self in the act of reading. You're right here, right now, experiencing the text... until a moment arrives when you're not. Sooner or later, that moment will come. A sound or smell will distract you. A stray thought will lead you into a thicket of ideas. You'll be snagged by sentiment, or caught up in a rush of feeling. That's okay. Once you notice the drift of your attention, you return to the page. *Gently*. Rather than blame or scold yourself for wandering off, you accept that it happened and bring yourself back.

We cultivate mindfulness throughout our days by returning to the present moment, again and again. This allows us to actually live our lives instead of just going through the motions. The more mindful we become over time, the happier we are. Studies reveal that regular mindfulness practice reduces stress, promotes health, stimulates learning and creativity, enhances relationships, helps us face suffering and loss, and strengthens our compassion for others.

Many resources for mindfulness practice quote snippets of poetry or even publish entire poems. The website of the Center for Mindfulness at the University of California San Diego, for instance, will provide you with links to dozens of poems used in its Mindfulness-Based Stress Reduction classes. Jon Kabat-Zinn, Sharon Salzberg, Joseph Goldstein and other esteemed mindfulness teachers regularly invoke poetry in their books and workshops. What accounts for this popular coupling of poetry and mindfulness?

As its very appearance makes plain, poetry invites a different kind of reading than prose. The white space around the text slows us down. Like an island on the page, its shape appeals to the eye. It begs for attention. It wants to be heard. When we choose to listen, we bring the poem to life. Our voice revels in the musicality, our breath is shaped by the lines. The imagery heightens our senses. The language revives our spirits.

The act of reading a poem—any poem—can therefore become an exercise in mindfulness. And our experience of the poem is magnified when its *subject* is particularly mindful. The poem might demonstrate what mindfulness is, recount an experience of it, or offer advice on how to practice it; perhaps it fleshes out a mindfulness theme, such as acceptance, impermanence, non-clinging ("letting go"), compassion, or the unity of all things. Such *mindfulness poems* inspire us to live better, and to make our world better; at the same time, they grant us a taste of being good enough, just as we are, in this world, just as it is.

Poetry of Presence contains over 150 mindfulness poems. Of course, you don't have to be interested in mindfulness to enjoy them. You can simply delight in their beautiful language, their vivid imagery, their uncommon wisdom. But if you sit down with this book in companionable silence, as with a cherished friend, the poems will teach you about mindfulness without your asking.

This collection is weighted toward English-language authors from North America and Europe because they're the poets with whom the two of us, as readers, are best acquainted. Still, its authors speak from a rich variety of backgrounds, perspectives and life-paths. Most are contemporary or recent poets. To some extent, all of them walk in the footsteps of great mindfulness poets of the more distant past, like Rainer Maria Rilke and Kahlil Gibran; or, even earlier, Rumi, Hafiz and Li Po. Older masters like these celebrated the divine presence hidden in the commonplace, or humanity's oneness with all that is. Though their worlds were vastly different from ours, their poetry still speaks to us today. We have presented a handful of their works, from gratitude.

The poems in this anthology aren't necessarily the "best" mindfulness poems out there. In the vast province of poetry, they're just ones we happen to like, and which, being skillfully crafted and highly accessible, are worthy representatives of the genre. Though their authors might never have heard of "mindfulness," they help us fathom it, and practice it. It's the nature of their craft to bear witness to the *here and now*. To compose a poem, after all, they must stop whatever else they're doing and give it their utter attention, start to finish. As Galway Kinnell once said, "[P]oetry is somebody standing up, so to speak, and saying, with as little concealment as possible, what it is for him or her to be on earth at this moment."

The authors who contributed to *Poetry of Presence* illuminate mindfulness in distinctive ways. Marilyn Nelson gives us a snapshot of what mindfulness isn't, then snaps us out of it. Craig Arnold describes how to eat a grapefruit with careful attention. Joyce Sutphen immerses us in the sensory details of a farm during summer. Wendell Berry instructs us on how to befriend silence and solitude. Jimmy Santiago Baca sings a praise song to the day. Richard Schiffman tells riddles. Mahmoud Darwish urges us to contemplate the adversities of others. Alice Walker affirms the value of "broken things," including ourselves. Lucille Clifton blesses us, sending us off on loving winds to "sail through this to that". . . . There are as many ways for poems to be mindful as there are poets.

An abundance of poems in this anthology, such as Seamus Heaney's "Postscript" and Mary Oliver's "When I Am Among the Trees," employ natural settings or imagery. As editors, we didn't set out to have so many, but we're not surprised this anthology mirrors who we are, what we value, and where we like to be. The fact is, we're women of the outdoors. Our daily lives are deeply informed by natural landscapes, flora and fauna, the ever-changing sky, and the rhythm of the seasons. We love digging in our gardens; watching thunderheads advance across the prairie; hiking back-country trails. With wind in our faces and dirt beneath our nails, the world seems simpler, focused. We're more at home.

For us, and perhaps for you as well, nature is a very effective mindfulness teacher. (Perhaps the best. Certainly the oldest.) Natural spaces sharpen our senses, help us tune in, make us more aware of being alive. As a result, we almost always relax, and decompress. We open, like sky. We slow down, like ground. We breathe freer. We talk less. All of this happens, well, *naturally*, without our having to try. As we transition from our doubts and worries, our gotta-dos and wanna-dos, into greater awareness, we feel more respect and gratitude for the natural world, more humility about our place in it, and more reverence for all life.

The question is, can we invest the same quality of mind that natural spaces inspire in the familiar settings of our everyday lives? It's one thing to practice mindfulness on a retreat into the mountains or an excursion along the beach. It's quite another to practice mindfulness smack dab in the middle of our busy lives, where there are hungry babies to feed, groceries to shop for, updates to post, a day's labor to perform, bills to pay, illnesses to endure, relationships to repair, injustices to remedy. . . . Mindfulness is tougher there. It requires clear intention. Patient discipline. Dedicated effort. So while this anthology is steeped in nature, it also has many poems that meet us *right where we are* and ask us to be more attentive and compassionate there, moment by moment, without passing judgment.

Whether or not we have a formal mindfulness practice, mindfulness poetry can help us keep (or regain) our footing in a world of tremendous upheaval. It can help prepare us to act with clarity amidst confusion, with lovingkindness amidst cruelty. It can also provide a refuge, where we can recharge when we're worn down, where we can just *be*.

"The invitation of poetry," according to Muriel Rukeyser, another of the authors in these pages, "is to bring your whole life to this moment. This moment is real, this moment is what we have . . . we are good poets inasmuch as we bring that invitation to you, and you are good readers inasmuch as you bring your whole life to the reading of the poem." As editors, we can't say it any better. *Bring your whole life—your whole being—to the poems in this book*. If you do, you'll magnify their expressive and transformative power.

Here's one approach to reading mindfully: First, pick a poem you'd like to savor. Because the poems in this collection are either brief or can be read in self-evident segments, they make excellent texts for focusing attention. Next, situate yourself in a comfortable time and place, free of distraction. Now stop. Relax. Breathe awhile. Summon your full awareness. When you're prepared, read the text, either silently or aloud. Notice when your mind wanders, and gently call it back. When you reach the end, sit with the poem for a spell. Don't analyze it. Don't judge it. Don't rush away from it. Just let it resonate, like the sounding of a bell, until it finishes with you.

We hope you'll return to *Poetry of Presence* again and again, as to the company of an old friend whose house you may enter without knocking. Each time you drop in, let the encounter be fresh. These poems are living texts. They change, because you do. Read each without judgment. Get to know it on its own terms while also sensing its resonance with other works. Refrain from asking, "Do I *like* this poem? It is better or worse than *that* one?" Just open yourself wide, like cloudless sky. Be the white space around the poem. The more welcoming you are of mindfulness poetry, and the more profoundly you engage with it, the more you'll be able to meet the world with a spirit of invitation, just as the poetry meets you.

Now the time has come to turn the page. Step into the company of these gifted poets. They have sought love and happiness, suffered hardships and grieved losses, just like you. Journey with them into the *here and now*. Offer your full presence to each moment, the only life that truly belongs to you. As the poets say, it's enough.

Phyllis Cole-Dai and Ruby Wilson

On How to Pick and Eat Poems

Phyllis Cole-Dai

Stop whatever it is you're doing.
Come down from the attic.
Grab a bucket or basket and head for light.
That's where the best poems grow, and in the dappled dark.

Go slow. Watch out for thorns and bears.
When you find a good bush, bow
to it, or take off your shoes.

Pluck. This poem. That poem. Any poem.
It should slip off the stem easy, just a little tickle.
No need to sniff first, judge the color, test the firmness—
you can only know it's ripe if you taste.

So put a poem upon your lips. Chew its pulp.
Let its juice spill over your tongue.
Let your reading of it teach you
what sort of creature you are
and the nature of the ground you walk upon.
Bring your whole life out loud to this one poem.
Eating one poem can save you, if you're hungry enough.

Take companions poem-picking when you can.
Visit wild and lovely and forgotten places, broken
and hidden and walled up spaces. Reach into brambles,
stain your skin, mash words against your teeth, for love.
And always leave some poems within easy reach for
the next picker, in kinship with the unknown.

If ever you carry away more poems than you need,
go on home to your kitchen, and make good jam.
Don't be in a rush, they're sure to keep.
Some will even taste better with age,
a rich batch of preserves.

Store up jars and jars of jam. Plenty for friends.
Plenty for the long, howling winter. Plenty for strangers.
Plenty for all the bread in this broken world.

The Poems

A Community of the Spirit

Rumi

There is a community of the spirit.
Join it, and feel the delight
of walking in the noisy street
and *being* the noise.

Drink *all* your passion,
and be a disgrace.

Close both eyes
to see with the other eye.

Open your hands,
if you want to be held.

Sit down in this circle.

Quit acting like a wolf, and feel
the shepherd's love filling you.

At night, your beloved wanders.
Don't accept consolations.

Close your mouth against food.
Taste the lover's mouth in yours.

You moan, "She left me." "He left me."
Twenty more will come.

Be empty of worrying.
Think of who created thought!

Why do you stay in prison
when the door is so wide open?

Move outside the tangle of fear-thinking.
Live in silence.

Flow down and down in always
widening rings of being.

Ancient Language

Hannah Stephenson

If you stand at the edge of the forest
and stare into it
every tree at the edge will blow a little extra
oxygen toward you

It has been proven
Leaves have admitted it

The pines I have known
have been especially candid

One said
that all breath in this world
is roped together

that breathing is
the most ancient language

Sifter

Naomi Shihab Nye

When our English teacher gave
our first writing invitation of the year,
Become a kitchen implement
in 2 descriptive paragraphs, I did not think
butcher knife or frying pan,
I thought immediately
of soft flour showering through the little holes
of the sifter and the sifter's pleasing circular
swishing sound, and wrote it down.
Rhoda became a teaspoon,
Roberto a funnel,
Jim a muffin tin
and Forrest a soup pot.
We read our paragraphs out loud.
Abby was a blender. Everyone laughed
and acted giddy but the more we thought about it,
we were all everything in the whole kitchen,
drawers and drainers,
singing teapot and grapefruit spoon
with serrated edges, we were all the
empty cup, the tray.
This, said our teacher, *is the beauty of metaphor.*
It opens doors.
What I could not know then
was how being a sifter
would help me all year long.
When bad days came
I would close my eyes and feel them passing
through the tiny holes.
When good days came
I would try to contain them gently
the way flour remains
in the sifter until you turn the handle.
Time, time. I was a sweet sifter in time
and no one ever knew.

The Way It Is

Lynn Ungar

One morning you might wake up
to realize that the knot in your stomach
had loosened itself and slipped away,
and that the pit of unfilled longing in your heart
had gradually, and without your really noticing,
been filled in—patched like a pothole, not quite
the same as it was, but good enough.

And in that moment it might occur to you
that your life, though not the way
you planned it, and maybe not even entirely
the way you wanted it, is nonetheless—
persistently, abundantly, miraculously—
exactly what it is.

Lie Down

Nancy Paddock

Lie down with your belly to the ground,
like an old dog in the sun. Smell
the greenness of the cloverleaf, feel the damp
earth through your clothes, let an ant
wander the uncharted territory
of your skin. Lie down
with your belly to the ground. Melt into
the earth's contours like a harmless snake.
All else is mere bravado.
Let your fists open into useless tendrils.
Let your mind resolve itself
in a tangle of grass.
Lie down with your belly
to the ground, flat out, on ground level.
Prostrate yourself before the soil
you will someday enter.
Stop doing.
Stop judging, fearing, trying.
This is not dying, but the way to live
in a world of change and gravity.
Let go. Let your burdens drop.
Let your grief-charge bleed off
into the ground.
Lie down with your belly to the ground
and then rise up
with the earth still in you.

The Patience of Ordinary Things

Pat Schneider

It is a kind of love, is it not?
How the cup holds the tea,
How the chair stands sturdy and foursquare,
How the floor receives the bottoms of shoes
Or toes. How soles of feet know
Where they're supposed to be.
I've been thinking about the patience
Of ordinary things, how clothes
Wait respectfully in closets
And soap dries quietly in the dish,
And towels drink the wet
From the skin of the back.
And the lovely repetition of stairs.
And what is more generous than a window?

Bali Hai Calls Mama

Marilyn Nelson

As I was putting away the groceries
I'd spent the morning buying
for the week's meals I'd planned
around things the baby could eat,
things my husband would eat,
and things I should eat
because they aren't too fattening,
late on a Saturday afternoon
after flinging my coat on a chair
and wiping the baby's nose
while asking my husband
what he'd fed it for lunch
and whether
the medicine I'd brought for him
had made his cough improve,
wiping the baby's nose again,
checking its diaper,
stepping over the baby
who was reeling to and from
the bottom kitchen drawer
with pots, pans, and plastic cups,
occasionally clutching the hem of my skirt
and whining to be held,
I was half listening for the phone
which never rings for me
to ring for me
and someone's voice to say that
I could forget about handing back
my students' exams which I'd had for a week,
that I was right about *The Waste Land*,
that I'd been given a raise,
all the time wondering
how my sister was doing,
whatever happened to my old lover(s),
and why my husband wanted
a certain brand of toilet paper;

and wished I hadn't, but I'd bought
another fashion magazine that promised
to make me beautiful by Christmas,
and there wasn't room for the creamed corn
and every time I opened the refrigerator door
the baby rushed to grab whatever was on the bottom shelf
which meant I constantly had to wrestle
jars of its mushy food out of its sticky hands
and I stepped on the baby's hand and the baby was screaming
and I dropped the bag of cake flour I'd bought to make cookies with
and my husband rushed in to find out what was wrong because the baby
was drowning out the sound of the touchdown although I had scooped
it up and was holding it in my arms so its crying was inside
my head like an echo in a barrel and I was running cold water
on its hand while somewhere in the back of my mind wondering what
to say about *The Waste Land* and whether I could get away with putting
broccoli in a meatloaf when

suddenly through the window
came the wild cry of geese.

The Second Music

Annie Lighthart

Now I understand that there are two melodies playing,
one below the other, one easier to hear, the other

lower, steady, perhaps more faithful for being less heard
yet always present.

When all other things seem lively and real,
this one fades. Yet the notes of it

touch as gently as fingertips, as the sound
of the names laid over each child at birth.

I want to stay in that music without striving or cover.
If the truth of our lives is what it is playing,

the telling is so soft
that this mortal time, this irrevocable change,

becomes beautiful. I stop and stop again
to hear the second music.

I hear the children in the yard, a train, then birds.
All this is in it and will be gone. I set my ear to it as I would to a heart.

Untitled

Gregory Orr

This is what was bequeathed us:
This earth the beloved left
And, leaving,
Left to us.

No other world
But this one:
Willows and the river
And the factory
With its black smokestacks.

No other shore, only this bank
On which the living gather.

No meaning but what we find here.
No purpose but what we make.

That, and the beloved's clear instructions:
Turn me into song; sing me awake.

A Little Stone in the Middle of the Road, in Florida

Muriel Rukeyser

My son as a child saying
God
is anything, even a little stone in the middle of the road, in
  Florida.
Yesterday
Nancy, my friend, after long illness:
You know what can lift me up, take me right out of despair?
No, what?
Anything.

Meditation on a Grapefruit

Craig Arnold

To wake when all is possible
before the agitations of the day
have gripped you
                To come to the kitchen
and peel a little basketball
for breakfast
          To tear the husk
like cotton padding   a cloud of oil
misting out of its pinprick pores
clean and sharp as pepper
                      To ease
each pale pink section out of its case
so carefully   without breaking
a single pearly cell
                To slide each piece
into a cold blue china bowl
the juice pooling   until the whole
fruit is divided from its skin
and only then to eat
              so sweet
                      a discipline
precisely pointless   a devout
involvement of the hands and senses
a pause   a little emptiness

each year harder to live within
each year harder to live without

The Cure for It All

Julia Fehrenbacher

Go gently today, don't hurry
or think about the next thing. Walk
with the quiet trees. Can you believe
how brave they are—how kind? Model your life
after theirs. Blow kisses
at yourself in the mirror

especially when
you think you've messed up. Forgive
yourself for not meeting your unreasonable
expectations. You are human, not
God—*don't be so arrogant.*

Praise fresh air,
clean water, good dogs. Spin
something from joy. Open
a window, even if
it's cold outside. Sit. Close
your eyes. Breathe. Allow

the river
of it all to pulse
through eyelashes,
fingertips, bare toes. Breathe in,
breathe out. Breathe until

you feel
your bigness, until the sun
rises in your veins. Breathe
until you stop needing
anything
to be different

The Word

Tony Hoagland

Down near the bottom
of the crossed-out list
of things you have to do today,

between "green thread"
and "broccoli," you find
that you have penciled "sunlight."

Resting on the page, the word
is beautiful. It touches you
as if you had a friend

and sunlight were a present
he had sent from someplace distant
as this morning—to cheer you up,

and to remind you that,
among your duties, pleasure
is a thing

that also needs accomplishing.
Do you remember?
that time and light are kinds

of love, and love
is no less practical
than a coffee grinder

or a safe spare tire?
Tomorrow you may be utterly
without a clue,

but today you get a telegram
from the heart in exile,
proclaiming that the kingdom

still exists,
the king and queen alive,
still speaking to their children,

—to any one among them
who can find the time
to sit out in the sun and listen.

Sunday Afternoon

Nancy Ann Schaefer

after Laura Van Prooyen

It's all so simple really. I stand
at the kitchen window peeling

potatoes. Red maple, white birch
border our patch, green and growing.

On the road, a John Deere tractor
sputters by, kicks up gravel and dust.

I can't see your eyes, shaded by
your Red Sox cap as you push

the mower in neat rows
across the lawn, seed the air

with the sweet scent of cut grass.
I dry my hands and cup a ladybug,

open the screen door to free her
outside on a bed of marigolds.

I hear the small birds
at the feeder. I hear song.

When I Am Among the Trees

Mary Oliver

When I am among the trees,
especially the willows and the honey locust,
equally the beech, the oaks and the pines,
they give off such hints of gladness.
I would almost say that they save me, and daily.

I am so distant from the hope of myself,
in which I have goodness, and discernment,
and never hurry through the world
  but walk slowly, and bow often.

Around me the trees stir in their leaves
and call out, "Stay awhile."
The light flows from their branches.

And they call again, "It's simple," they say,
"and you, too, have come
into the world to do this, to go easy, to be filled
with light, and to shine."

Praise Song

Barbara Crooker

Praise the light of late November,
the thin sunlight that goes deep in the bones.
Praise the crows chattering in the oak trees;
though they are clothed in night, they do not
despair. Praise what little there's left:
the small boats of milkweed pods, husks, hulls,
shells, the architecture of trees. Praise the meadow
of dried weeds: yarrow, goldenrod, chicory,
the remains of summer. Praise the blue sky
that hasn't cracked yet. Praise the sun slipping down
behind the beechnuts, praise the quilt of leaves
that covers the grass: Scarlet Oak, Sweet Gum,
Sugar Maple. Though darkness gathers, praise our crazy
fallen world; it's all we have, and it's never enough.

Lessons from Darkness

Anita Barrows

> *"I'm afraid of the darkness, and the hole in it;*
> *and I see it sometime of every day!"*
> —Martin Luther, in *Luther*

Everything you love will perish. Try saying this to yourself
at breakfast, watching the amber-colored tea
swirl in the teapot. Try it on the tree, the clouds, the dog
asleep under the table, the sparrow taking a bath
in the neighbor's gutter. A magician's act: *Presto!*
On a morning you feel open enough to embrace it
imagine it gone. Then pack the child's lunch: smooth the thick
peanut butter, the jeweled raspberry preserves,
over the bread. Tell yourself the world
must go on forever. This is why
you feed her, imagining the day—orderly—
unfolding, imagining what you teach her
is true. Is something she will use. This is why, later, you will go out
into the garden, among the calendula, rosemary, hibiscus,
run your finger along the trunk of hawthorn
as though it were the body
of a lover, thinking of the child
on the steps of the schoolyard, eating her sandwich. Thinking *nothing,*
transparent air, where her hands are.

Thinking

Danusha Laméris

Don't you wish they would stop, all the thoughts
swirling around in your head, bees in a hive, dancers
tapping their way across the stage? I should rake the leaves
in the carport, buy Christmas lights. Was there really life on Mars?
What will I cook for dinner? I walk up the driveway,
put out the garbage bins. I should stop using plastic bags,
visit my friend whose husband just left her for the Swedish nanny.
I wish I hadn't said Patrick's painting looked "ominous."
Maybe that's why he hasn't called. Does the car need oil again?
There's a hole in the ozone the size of Texas and everything
seems to be speeding up. Come, let's stand by the window
and look out at the light on the field. Let's watch how the clouds
cover the sun and almost nothing stirs in the grass.

The Quiet Listeners

Laura Foley

Go into the woods
and tell your story
to the trees.
They are wise
standing in their folds of silence
among white crystals of rock
and dying limbs.
And they have time.
Time for the swaying of leaves,
the floating down,
the dust.
They have time for gathering
and holding the earth about their feet.
Do this.
It is something I have learned.
How they will bend down to you
softly.
They will bend down to you
and listen.

Lost

David Wagoner

Stand still. The trees ahead and bushes beside you
Are not lost. Wherever you are is called Here,
And you must treat it as a powerful stranger,
Must ask permission to know it and be known.
The forest breathes. Listen. It answers,
I have made this place around you.
If you leave it, you may come back again, saying Here.
No two trees are the same to Raven.
No two branches are the same to Wren.
If what a tree or a bush does is lost on you,
You are surely lost. Stand still. The forest knows
Where you are. You must let it find you.

Blackbirds

Julie Cadwallader Staub

I am 52 years old, and have spent
truly the better part
of my life out-of-doors
but yesterday I heard a new sound above my head
a rustling, ruffling quietness in the spring air

and when I turned my face upward
I saw a flock of blackbirds
rounding a curve I didn't know was there
and the sound was simply all those wings,
all those feathers against air, against gravity
and such a beautiful winning:
the whole flock taking a long, wide turn
as if of one body and one mind.

How do they *do* that?

If we lived only in human society
what a puny existence that would be

but instead we live and move and have our being
here, in this curving and soaring world
that is not our own
so that when mercy and tenderness triumph in our lives
and when, even more rarely, we unite and move together
toward a common good,

we can think to ourselves:

ah yes, this is how it's meant to be.

We Are of a Tribe

Alberto Ríos

We plant seeds in the ground
And dreams in the sky,

Hoping that, someday, the roots of one
Will meet the upstretched limbs of the other.

It has not happened yet.
We share the sky, all of us, the whole world:

Together, we are a tribe of eyes that look upward,
Even as we stand on uncertain ground.

The earth beneath us moves, quiet and wild,
Its boundaries shifting, its muscles wavering.

The dream of sky is indifferent to all this,
Impervious to borders, fences, reservations.

The sky is our common home, the place we all live.
There we are in the world together.

The dream of sky requires no passport.
Blue will not be fenced. Blue will not be a crime.

Look up. Stay awhile. Let your breathing slow.
Know that you always have a home here.

Untitled

Kabir

The Guest is inside you, and also inside me;
    you know the sprout is hidden inside the seed.
We are all struggling; none of us has gone far.
Let your arrogance go, and look around inside.

The blue sky opens out further and farther,
the daily sense of failure goes away,
the damage I have done to myself fades,
a million suns come forward with light,
when I sit firmly in that world.

I hear bells ringing that no one has shaken,
inside "love" there is more joy than we know of,
rain pours down, although the sky is clear of clouds,
there are whole rivers of light.
The universe is shot through in all parts by a single sort of love.
How hard it is to feel that joy in all our four bodies!

Those who hope to be reasonable about it fail.
The arrogance of reason has separated us from that love.
With the word "reason" you already feel miles away.

How lucky Kabir is, that surrounded by all this joy
he sings inside his own little boat.
His poems amount to one soul meeting another.
These songs are about forgetting dying and loss.
They rise above both coming in and going out.

Take Love for Granted

Jack Ridl

Assume it's in the kitchen,
under the couch, high
in the pine tree out back,
behind the pile of shoes,
in the wood stove. Don't
try proving your love
is bigger than the Grand
Canyon, the Milky Way,
the urban sprawl of L.A.
Take it for granted. Take it
out with the garbage. Bring it
in with the take out. Take
it for a walk. Wake it
every day, say, "Good
morning." Then make
the coffee. Warm the cups.
Don't expect much
of the day. Be glad when
you make it back to bed.
Say Yes when he says he'll
be home by six from
the Duck Barn and
wanders through
the door at midnight.
Say Yes when she says she'll
be home by six from her
studio and wanders through
the door at midnight.
Be glad he threw out that
box of old whatever they were.
Be glad she leaves her shoes
in the way. Snow will come.
Spring will show up.
Summer will be humid.

The leaves will fall
in the fall. That's more
than you need. We can
love anybody, even
everybody. But you
can love each other,
the silence, the sighing,
and saying to yourself,
"That's her." "That's him."
Then to each other, "I know!
Let's go out for breakfast!"

Love After Love

Derek Walcott

The time will come
when, with elation
you will greet yourself arriving
at your own door, in your own mirror
and each will smile at the other's welcome,

and say, sit here. Eat.
You will love again the stranger who was your self.
Give wine. Give bread. Give back your heart
to itself, to the stranger who has loved you

all your life, whom you ignored
for another, who knows you by heart.
Take down the love letters from the bookshelf

the photographs, the desperate notes,
peel your own image from the mirror.
Sit. Feast on your life.

A Sacrament

Paulann Petersen

Become that high priest,
the bee. Drone your way
from one fragrant
temple to another, nosing
into each altar. Drink
what's divine—
and while you're there,
let some of the sacred
cling to your limbs.
Wherever you go
leave a small trail
of its golden crumbs.

In your wake
the world unfolds
its rapture, the fruit
of its blooming.
Rooms in your house
fill with that sweetness
your body both
makes and eats.

This Morning

David Budbill

Oh, this life,
the now,
this morning,

which I
can turn
into forever

by simply
loving
what is here,

is gone
by noon.

In the Middle

Barbara Crooker

of a life that's as complicated as everyone else's,
struggling for balance, juggling time.
The mantle clock that was my grandfather's
has stopped at 9:20; we haven't had time
to get it repaired. The brass pendulum is still,
the chimes don't ring. One day I look out the window,
green summer, the next, the leaves have already fallen,
and a grey sky lowers the horizon. Our children almost grown,
our parents gone, it happened so fast. Each day, we must learn
again how to love, between morning's quick coffee
and evening's slow return. Steam from a pot of soup rises,
mixing with the yeasty smell of baking bread. Our bodies
twine, and the big black dog pushes his great head between;
his tail, a metronome, 3/4 time. We'll never get there,
Time is always ahead of us, running down the beach, urging
us on faster, faster, but sometimes we take off our watches,
sometimes we lie in the hammock, caught between the mesh
of rope and the net of stars, suspended, tangled up
in love, running out of time.

Brotherhood

Octavio Paz

Homage to Claudius Ptolemy

I am a man: little do I last
and the night is enormous.
But I look up:
the stars write.
Unknowing I understand:
I too am written,
and at this very moment
someone spells me out.

Under Ideal Conditions

Al Zolynas

say in the flattest part of North Dakota
on a starless moonless night
no breath of wind

a man could light a candle
then walk away
every now and then
he could turn and see
the candle burning

seventeen miles later
provided conditions remained ideal
he could still see the flame

somewhere between the seventeenth and eighteenth mile
he would lose the light

if he were walking backwards
he would know the exact moment
when he lost the flame

he could step forward and find it again
back and forth
dark to light light to dark

what's the place where the light disappears?
where the light reappears?
don't tell me about photons
and eyeballs
reflection and refraction
don't tell me about one hundred and eighty-six thousand
miles per second and the theory of relativity

all I know is that place
where the light appears and disappears
that's the place where we live

Prayer for the Dead

Stuart Kestenbaum

The light snow started late last night and continued
all night long while I slept and could hear it occasionally
enter my sleep, where I dreamed my brother
was alive again and possessing the beauty of youth, aware
that he would be leaving again shortly and that is the lesson
of the snow falling and of the seeds of death that are in everything
that is born: we are here for a moment
of a story that is longer than all of us and few of us
remember, the wind is blowing out of someplace
we don't know, and each moment contains rhythms
within rhythms, and if you discover some old piece
of your own writing, or an old photograph,
you may not remember that it was you and even if it was once you,
it's not you now, not this moment that the synapses fire
and your hands move to cover your face in a gesture
of grief and remembrance.

a song with no end

Charles Bukowski

when Whitman wrote, "I sing the body electric"

I know what he
meant
I know what he
wanted:

to be completely alive every moment
in spite of the inevitable.

we can't cheat death but we can make it
work so hard
that when it does take
us

it will have known a victory just as
perfect as
ours.

Longing

Julie Cadwallader Staub

Consider the blackpoll warbler.

She tips the scales
at one ounce
before she migrates, taking off
from the seacoast to our east
flying higher and higher

ascending two or three miles
during her eighty hours of flight
until she lands,
in Tobago,
north of Venezuela
three days older,
and weighing half as much.

She flies over open ocean almost the whole way.

She is not so different from us.
The arc of our lives is a mystery too.
We do not understand,
we cannot see
what guides us on our way:
that longing that pulls us toward light.

Not knowing, we fly onward
hearing the dull roar of the waves below.

Afterwards

William Stafford

Mostly you look back and say, “Well, OK. Things might have
been different, sure, and it’s too bad, but look—
things happen like that, and you did what you could.”
You go back and pick up the pieces. There’s tomorrow.
There’s that long bend in the river on the way
home. Fluffy bursts of milkweed are floating
through shafts of sunlight or disappearing where
trees reach out from their deep dark roots.

Maybe people have to go in and out of shadows
till they learn that floating, that immensity
waiting to receive whatever arrives with trust.
Maybe somebody has to explore what happens
when one of us wanders over near the edge
and falls for awhile. Maybe it was your turn.

Still Life at Dusk

Rosemerry Wahtola Trommer

It happens surprisingly fast,
the way your shadow leaves you.

All day you've been linked by
the light, but now that darkness

gathers the world in a great black tide,
your shadow joins

the sea of all other shadows.
If you stand here long enough,

you, too, will forget your lines
and merge with the tall grass and

old trees, with the crows and the
flooding river—all these pieces

of the world that daylight has broken
into objects of singular loneliness.

It happens surprisingly fast, the drawing in
of your shadow, and standing

in the field, you become the field,
and standing in the night, you

are gathered by night. Invisible
birds sing to the memory of light

but then even those separate songs fade,
tiny drops of ink in an infinite spilling.

Getting up Early

Anne Porter

Just as the night was fading
Into the dusk of morning
When the air was cool as water
When the town was quiet
And I could hear the sea

I caught sight of the moon
No higher than the roof-tops
Our neighbor the moon

An hour before the sunrise
She glowed with her own sunrise
Gold in the grey of morning

World without town or forest
Without wars or sorrows
She paused between two trees

And it was as if in secret
Not wanting to be seen
She chose to visit us
So early in the morning.

Testimony

Rebecca Baggett

for my daughters

I want to tell you
that the world is still beautiful.
I tell you that despite
children raped on city streets,
shot down in school rooms,
despite the slow poisons seeping
from old and hidden sins
into our air, soil, water,
despite the thinning film
that encloses our aching world.
Despite my own terror and despair.

I want you to look again and again,
to recognize the tender grasses,
curled like a baby's fine hairs
around your fingers, as a recurring
miracle, to see that the river rocks
shine like God, that the crisp
voices of the orange and gold
October leaves are laughing at death.
I want you to look beneath
the grass, to note
the fragile hieroglyphs
of ant, snail, beetle. I want
you to understand that you are
no more and no less necessary
than the brown recluse, the ruby-
throated hummingbird, the humpback
whale, the profligate mimosa.

I want to say, like Neruda,
that I am waiting for
"a great and common tenderness,"

that I still believe
we are capable of attention,
that anyone who notices the world
must want to save it.

A Gift

Denise Levertov

Just when you seem to yourself
nothing but a flimsy web
of questions, you are given
the questions of others to hold
in the emptiness of your hands,
songbird eggs that can still hatch
if you keep them warm,
butterflies opening and closing themselves
in your cupped palms, trusting you not to injure
their scintillant fur, their dust.
You are given the questions of others
as if they were answers
to all you ask. Yes, perhaps
this gift is your answer.

What's in the Temple?

Tom Barrett

In the quiet spaces of my mind a thought lies still, but ready to spring.
It begs me to open the door so it can walk about.
The poets speak in obscure terms, pointing madly at the unsayable.
The sages say nothing, but walk ahead, patting their thigh, calling for us
to follow.
The monk sits pen in hand, poised to explain the cloud of unknowing.
The seeker seeks, just around the corner from the truth.
If she stands still, it will catch up with her.

Pause with us here awhile.
Put your ear to the wall of your heart.
Listen for the whisper of knowing there.
Love will touch you if you are very still.

If I say the word *God*, people run away.
They've been frightened, sat upon till the spirit cried *uncle*.
Now they play hide and seek with somebody they can't name.
They know God's out there looking for them, and they want to be found,
but there is all this stuff in the way.

I can't talk about God and make any sense,
and I can't not talk about God and make any sense.
So you and I talk about the weather, and we are talking about God.

I miss the old temples where we could hang out with God.
Still, we have pet pounds where we can feel love draped in warm fur,
and sense the whole tragedy of life and death.
We can see there the consequences of carelessness,
and feel there the yapping urgency of life that wants to be lived.
The only things lacking are the frankincense and myrrh.

We don't build many temples anymore.
Maybe we learned that the sacred can't be contained.
Or maybe it can't be sustained inside a building.
Buildings crumble.
It's the spirit that lives on.

If you had a temple in the secret spaces of your heart,
what would you worship there?
What would you bring to sacrifice?
What would be behind the curtain in the holy of holies?

Go there now.
Look behind the curtain.

Lakol Wicoun

Lydia Whirlwind Soldier

I retreat to the edge of dreams
empty my heart of haunting fears
I fly with the red-tail hawk
along the bank of rolling thunderheads
into the mysteries of prayer
"There is no word for religion"
Grandpa said
"It is Lakol Wicoun drawn
from that blade of grass,
even from that tiny ant
carrying its burden,
it is in the memory of the
buffalo, the elk, coyote,
the eagle and the bear
yes, even the butterfly
it is in our laws, unwritten
given by Unci Maka,
from the stars and
from the pull of the moon
it lives in the mountains,
the prairies and in the water
it rides on each snowflake
and in the shadow of our
language
it is the center, our center
where sin, guilt and
redemption do not own us
Takoja, remember to return
to that center
honor the silence
where the life force
whispers in the wind
and tells
the story of our people."

For a brief note regarding the cultural context of this poem, see Notes on the Poems.

Visiting Mountains

Ted Kooser

The plains ignore us,
but these mountains listen,
an audience of thousands
holding its breath
in each rock. Climbing,
we pick our way
over the skulls of small talk.
On the prairies below us,
the grass leans this way and that
in discussion;
words fly away like corn shucks
over the fields.
Here, lost in a mountain's
attention, there's nothing to say.

A Brief Détente

Rosemerry Wahtola Trommer

From across the pond,
the doe and I regard each other—
she with enormous brown eyes,

I with my hands full of empty.
We take turns pretending
we're not watching each other,

but we are, aware
of each other's slightest move.
She goes back to her eating.

I go back to shaking
the dried iris pods
to see if they rattle. They do.

She startles
but does not run to the trees.
I am oddly relieved

as she interests herself again
in the grass spiking out of the snow.
All day a feeling of doom

has settled in me, a heavy,
unshakable dark. It doesn't lessen
because of the doe, but perhaps

it does. She lifts her head again
for something I do not hear or see,
and I, too, tense before we return

to the fragile moment, this small act
of trusting each other, witnesses
to the cold in the air,

the ice already cured on the pond,
the day losing
whatever color it had left,

the iris seeds spilling
their dark, latent praise
atop the snow.

Love for Other Things

Tom Hennen

It's easy to love a deer
But try to care about bugs and scrawny trees
Love the puddle of lukewarm water
From last week's rain.
Leave the mountains alone for now.
Also the clear lakes surrounded by pines.
People are lined up to admire them.
Get close to the things that slide away in the dark.
Be grateful even for the boredom
That sometimes seems to involve the whole world.
Think of the frost
That will crack our bones eventually.

The Offering

Laura Foley

These woods
on the edges of a lake
are settling now
to winter darkness.
Whatever was going to die
is gone—
crickets, ferns, swampgrass.
Bare earth fills long spaces of a field.
But look—
a single oak leaf
brown and shining
like a leather purse.
See what it so delicately offers,
lying upturned on the path.
See how it reflects in its opened palm
a cup of deep, unending sky.

The Bare Arms of Trees

John Tagliabue

Sometimes when I see the bare arms of trees in the evening
I think of men who have died without love,
Of desolation and space between branch and branch,
I think of immovable whiteness and lean coldness and fear
And the terrible longing between people stretched apart as these
 branches
And the cold space between.
I think of the vastness and courage between this step and that step
Of the yearning and the fear of the meeting, of the terrible desire
 held apart.
I think of the ocean of longing that moves between land and land
And between people, the space and ocean.
The bare arms of the trees are immovable, without the play of leaves,
 without the sound of wind;
I think of the unseen love and the unknown thoughts that exist
 between tree and tree
As I pass these things in the evening, as I walk.

Still

A. R. Ammons

I said I will find what is lowly
      and put the roots of my identity
      down there:
each day I'll wake up
and find the lowly nearby,
      a handy focus and reminder,
a ready measure of my significance,
the voice by which I would be heard,
the wills, the kinds of selfishness
      I could
freely adopt as my own:

but though I have looked everywhere,
      I can find nothing
      to give myself to:
      everything is

magnificent with existence, is in
surfeit of glory:
nothing is diminished,
nothing has been diminished for me:

I said what is more lowly than the grass:
      ah, underneath,
      a ground-crust of dry-burnt moss:
      I looked at it closely
and said this can be my habitat: but
nestling in I
found
      below the brown exterior
      green mechanisms beyond the intellect
awaiting resurrection in rain: so I got up

and ran saying there is nothing lowly in the universe:
I found a beggar:
he had stumps for legs: nobody was paying
him any attention: everybody went on by:
        I nestled in and found his life:
there, love shook his body like a devastation
I said
        though I have looked everywhere
        I can find nothing lowly
        in the universe:

I whirled though transfigurations up and down,
transfigurations of size and shape and place:
        at one sudden point came still,
        stood in wonder:
moss, beggar, weed, tick, pine, self, magnificent
        with being!

The Owl Cries at Night

Freya Manfred

The owl cries at night,
and I imagine her wide gold eyes
and feathered ears tuned
to the trembling woods and waters,
seeing and hearing what
I will never see or hear:
a red fox with one bloody paw,
a hunch-backed rabbit running,
sand grains grating on the shore,
a brown leaf crackling
under a brown mouse foot.
With so much to learn,
I could stop writing forever,
and still live well.

Fluent

John O'Donohue

I would love to live
Like a river flows,
Carried by the surprise
Of its own unfolding.

Midlife

Julie Cadwallader Staub

This is as far as the light
of my understanding
has carried me:
        an October morning
        a canoe built by hand
        a quiet current

above me the trees arc
green and golden
against a cloudy sky

below me the river responds
with perfect reflection
a hundred feet deep
a hundred feet high.

To take a cup of this river
to drink its purple and gray
its golden and green

to see
a bend in the river up ahead
and still
say
yes.

This Day

Jimmy Santiago Baca

I feel foolish,
  like those silly robins jumping on the ditch boughs
  when I run by them.
        Those robins do not have the grand style of the red tailed hawk,
        no design, no dream, just robins acting stupid.
They've never smoked cigarettes, drank whiskey, consumed drugs
as I have.
        In their mindless
        fluttering about
        filled with nonsense,
          they tell me how they
            love the Great Spirit,
        scold me not to be self-pitying,
        to open my life
        and make this day a bough on a tree
        leaning over infinity, where eternity flows forward
        and with day the river runs
            carrying all that falls in it.
        Be happy Jimmy, they chirp,
        Jimmy, be silly, make this day a tree
        leaning over the river eternity
        and fuss about in its branches.

Versions of Ghalib: Ghazal I

Ghalib

i
Everything sings, in each moment, a song—and is,
in the very next moment, unsung.

It's no use being a mirror which sees both sides;
both sides are wrong.

What you claim to know will fail you; so will
what you venerate. Drink up. Refill your cup.

Deliberately love kicks up dust
to irritate the eye between two worlds.

ii
Each song loves and hates itself.
If there's a mirror which tells the difference, don't look.

Forget what you know; don't bother to believe.
Not-knowing is the only cup which can hold the world.

Where love has been and gone, the world grows honest.
Each thing sings: *I am essential. I do not exist.*

All you think you know is wrong. So is all you worship.
No matter how much you drink, there's more in the cup.

iii
Praise the futility of song. Accept that the shine in the mirror
is wrong. You are not important.

What's a mirror, anyway? Who looks back from that bright glass?
It's love again, come to save us, or drive us mad.

The more you know, the less you see;
faith can't be drunk, though it fills your cup.

Love's like a dust which settles on all things
and clings like skin. Even the sky bows down to it.

For a brief note regarding the cultural context of this poem, see Notes on the Poems.

A Momentary Creed

W. S. Merwin

I believe in the ordinary day
that is here at this moment and is me

I do not see it going its own way
but I never saw how it came to me

it extends beyond whatever I may
think I know and all that is real to me

it is the present that it bears away
where has it gone when it has gone from me

there is no place I know outside today
except for the unknown all around me

the only presence that appears to stay
everything that I call mine it lent me

even the way that I believe the day
for as long as it is here and is me

Because even the word *obstacle* is an obstacle

Alison Luterman

Try to love everything that gets in your way:
the Chinese women in flowered bathing caps
murmuring together in Mandarin, doing leg exercises in your lane
while you execute thirty-six furious laps,
one for every item on your to-do list.
The heavy-bellied man who goes thrashing through the water
like a horse with a harpoon stuck in its side,
whose breathless tsunamis rock you from your course.
Teachers all. Learn to be small
and swim through obstacles like a minnow
without grudges or memory. Dart
toward your goal, sperm to egg. Thinking *Obstacle*
is another obstacle. Try to love the teenage girl
lounging idly against the ladder, showing off her new tattoo:
Cette vie est la mienne, This life is mine,
in thick blue-black letters on her ivory instep.
Be glad she'll have that to look at all her life,
and keep going, keep going. Swim by an uncle
in the lane next to yours who is teaching his nephew
how to hold his breath underwater,
even though kids aren't allowed at this hour. Someday,
years from now, this boy
who is kicking and flailing in the exact place
you want to touch and turn
will be a young man at a wedding on a boat,
raising his champagne glass in a toast,
when a huge wave hits, washing everyone overboard.
He'll come up coughing and spitting like he is now,
but he'll come up like a cork,
alive. So your moment
of impatience must bow in service to a larger story,
because if something is in your way it is
going your way, the way
of all beings; towards darkness, towards light.

Mind Wanting More

Holly J. Hughes

Only a beige slat of sun
above the horizon, like a shade
pulled not quite down. Otherwise,
clouds. Sea rippled here and
there. Birds reluctant to fly.
The mind wants a shaft of sun to
stir the grey porridge of clouds,
an osprey to stitch sea to sky
with its barred wings, some dramatic
music: a symphony, perhaps
a Chinese gong.

But the mind always
wants more than it has—
one more bright day of sun,
one more clear night in bed
with the moon; one more hour
to get the words right; one
more chance for the heart in hiding
to emerge from its thicket
in dried grasses—as if this quiet day
with its tentative light weren't enough,
as if joy weren't strewn all around.

Instructions

Sheri Hostetler

Give up the world; give up self; finally, give up God.
Find God in rhododendrons and rocks,
passers-by, your cat.
Pare your beliefs, your Absolutes.
Make it simple; make it clean.
No carry-on luggage allowed.
Examine all you have
with a loving and critical eye, then
throw away some more.
Repeat. Repeat.
Keep this and only this:
    what your heart beats loudly for
    what feels heavy and full in your gut.
There will only be one or two
things you will keep,
and they will fit lightly
in your pocket.

Stone

Danusha Laméris

And what am I doing here, in a yurt on the side of a hill
at the ragged edge of the tree line, sheltered by conifer and bay,
watching the wind lift, softly, the dry leaves of bamboo?
I lie on the floor and let the sun fall across my back,
as I have been for the past hour, listening to the distant traffic,
to the calls of birds I cannot name. Once, I had so much
I wanted to accomplish. Now, all I know is that I want
to get closer to it—to the rocky slope, the orange petals
of the nasturtium adorning the fence, the wind's sudden breath.
Close enough that I can almost feel, at night, the slight pressure
of the stars against my skin. Isn't this what the mystics meant
when they spoke of forsaking the world? Not to turn our backs to it,
only to its elaborate plots, its complicated pleasures—
in favor of the pine's long shadow, the slow song of the grass.
I'm always forgetting, and remembering, and forgetting.
I want to leave something here in the rough dirt: a twig,
a small stone—perhaps this poem—a reminder to begin,
again, by listening carefully with the body's rapt attention
—remember? To *this*, to *this*.

The Mosquito Among the Raindrops

Teddy Macker

The mosquito among the raindrops...
It's equivalent to getting hit, says the scientist, by a falling school bus.
And hit every twenty seconds.

And the mosquito lives.

In fact, she doesn't even try to avoid the drops.
No zigzagging, no ducking. No hiding under eaves.

How does she do it?

No resistance to the force.

She hitches a ride on the blow,
a stowaway on that which brings her down.

She becomes "one with the drop,"
knowing that to fly again

she must fall.

One Heart

Li-Young Lee

Look at the birds. Even flying
is born

out of nothing. The first sky
is inside you, open

at either end of day.
The work of wings

was always freedom, fastening
one heart to every falling thing.

Winter Poem

Nikki Giovanni

once a snowflake fell
on my brow and i loved
it so much and i kissed
it and it was happy and called its cousins
and brothers and a web
of snow engulfed me then
i reached to love them all
and i squeezed them and they became
a spring rain and i stood perfectly
still and was a flower

Camas Lilies

Lynn Ungar

Consider the lilies of the field,
the blue banks of camas opening
into acres of sky along the road.
Would the longing to lie down
and be washed by that beauty
abate if you knew their usefulness,
how the natives ground their bulbs
for flour, how the settlers' hogs
uprooted them, grunting in gleeful
oblivion as the flowers fell?

And you—what of your rushed
and useful life? Imagine setting it all down—
papers, plans, appointments, everything—
leaving only a note: "Gone
to the fields to be lovely. Be back
when I'm through with blooming."

Even now, unneeded and uneaten,
the camas lilies gaze out above the grass
from their tender blue eyes.
Even in sleep your life will shine.
Make no mistake. Of course
your work will always matter.
Yet Solomon in all his glory
was not arrayed like one of these.

Saint Francis and the Sow

Galway Kinnell

The bud
stands for all things,
even for those things that don't flower,
for everything flowers, from within, of self-blessing;
though sometimes it is necessary
to reteach a thing its loveliness,
to put a hand on its brow
of the flower
and retell it in words and in touch
it is lovely
until it flowers again from within, of self-blessing;
as Saint Francis
put his hand on the creased forehead
of the sow, and told her in words and in touch
blessings of earth on the sow, and the sow
began remembering all down her thick length,
from the earthen snout all the way
through the fodder and slops to the spiritual curl of the tail,
from the hard spininess spiked out from the spine
down through the great broken heart
to the blue milken dreaminess spurting and shuddering
from the fourteen teats into the fourteen mouths sucking and blowing
beneath them:
the long, perfect loveliness of sow.

Evening Star

Charles Goodrich

Fork down hay
for the white-face steers.
Sit in the hay mow door
watching the horses graze,
chewing myself a dry clover sprig.

Long day over.
No evening plans.
Dust motes drift
on the ambering light.
Pigeons flap and coo in the rafters.

First star now
low in the east.
Sweat cools
and crusts on my face,
muscles lean back on their bones

and all thoughts heal down
to a low whistling.

Miracle Fair

Wislawa Szymborska

Commonplace miracle:
that so many commonplace miracles happen.

An ordinary miracle:
in the dead of night
the barking of invisible dogs.

One miracle out of many:
a small, airy cloud
yet it can block a large and heavy moon.

Several miracles in one:
an alder tree reflected in the water,
and that it's backwards left to right
and that it grows there, crown down
and never reaches the bottom,
even though the water is shallow.

An everyday miracle:
winds weak to moderate
turning gusty in storms.

First among equal miracles:
cows are cows.

Second to none:
just this orchard
from just that seed.

A miracle without a cape and top hat:
scattering white doves.

A miracle, for what else could you call it:
today the sun rose at three-fourteen
and will set at eight-o-one.

A miracle, less surprising than it should be:
even though the hand has fewer than six fingers,
it still has more than four.

A miracle, just take a look around:
the world is everywhere.

An additional miracle, as everything is additional:
the unthinkable
is thinkable.

Feather at Midday

Sister Dang Nghiem

If I had not stopped to watch
a feather flying by,
I would not have seen its landing—
a tiny pure white feather.

Gently, I blew a soft breath
to send it back to the spring.

If I had not looked up to watch
the feather gliding over the roof,
I would not have seen
the crescent moon
hanging at midday.

(Spring 2001)

Postscript

Seamus Heaney

And some time make the time to drive out west
Into County Clare, along the Flaggy Shore,
In September or October, when the wind
And the light are working off each other
So that the ocean on one side is wild
With foam and glitter, and inland among stones
The surface of a slate-grey lake is lit
By the earthed lightning of a flock of swans,
Their feathers roughed and ruffling, white on white,
Their fully grown headstrong-looking heads
Tucked or cresting or busy underwater.
Useless to think you'll park and capture it
More thoroughly. You are neither here nor there,
A hurry through which known and strange things pass
As big soft buffetings come at the car sideways
And catch the heart off guard and blow it open.

The Muse Is a Little Girl

Marjorie Saiser

The muse is a little girl, impossibly polite.
She arrives when you're talking
or walking away from your car.
She's barefoot, she stands
next to you, mute; she taps your sleeve,
not even on your skin, just touches the cloth
of your plaid shirt, touches it twice.
She feels with her index finger the texture
and you keep talking, or you don't.
She will wait one minute. She is not hungry
or unhappy or poor. She goes somewhere else
unless you turn and look at her
and write it down. I'm kidding.
She's a horse you want to ride, she's a tall horse,
she's heavy, as if she could bear armor.
You can't catch her with apples.
I don't know how you get on.
I remember my cold fingers in the black mane.

How to Be a Poet

Wendell Berry

(to remind myself)

Make a place to sit down.
Sit down. Be quiet.
You must depend upon
affection, reading, knowledge,
skill—more of each
than you have—inspiration,
work, growing older, patience,
for patience joins time
to eternity. Any readers
who like your work,
doubt their judgment.

Breathe with unconditional breath
the unconditioned air.
Shun electric wire.
Communicate slowly. Live
a three-dimensioned life;
stay away from screens.
Stay away from anything
that obscures the place it is in.
There are no unsacred places;
there are only sacred places
and desecrated places.

Accept what comes from silence.
Make the best you can of it.
Of the little words that come
out of the silence, like prayers
prayed back to the one who prays,
make a poem that does not disturb
the silence from which it came.

Keeping quiet

Pablo Neruda

Now we will count to twelve
and we will all keep still.

For once on the face of the earth,
let's not speak in any language;
let's stop for one second,
and not move our arms so much.

It would be an exotic moment
without rush, without engines;
we would all be together
in a sudden strangeness.

Fishermen in the cold sea
would not harm whales
and the man gathering salt
would look at his hurt hands.

Those who prepare green wars,
wars with gas, wars with fire,
victories with no survivors,
would put on clean clothes
and walk about with their brothers
in the shade, doing nothing.

What I want should not be confused
with total inactivity.
Life is what it is about;
I want no truck with death.

If we were not so single-minded
about keeping our lives moving,
and for once could do nothing,
perhaps a huge silence
might interrupt this sadness
of never understanding ourselves
and of threatening ourselves with death.

Perhaps the earth can teach us
as when everything seems dead
and later proves to be alive.

Now I'll count up to twelve
and you keep quiet and I will go.

On the Necessity of Snow Angels for the Well-Being of the World

Grace Butcher

Wherever there is snow, I go,
making angels along the way.
Luckily angels have no gender
and are easier to make
than you might think.

All you have to do is let go,
fall on your back,
look up at the sky as if in prayer.
Move your arms like wings.
Move your legs to make a robe.
Rise carefully so as to do no harm,
and walk away.

All the angels along the path behind you
will sparkle in sunlight, gleam under the stars.
In spring the angels will be invisible
but really they are still there,
their outlines remain on the earth
where you put them, waiting
for you and the snow to return.

Keep walking,
towards the next beautiful thing
you will do.

When I Taught Her How to Tie Her Shoes

Penny Harter

A revelation, the student
in high school who didn't know
how to tie her shoes.

I took her into the book-room, knowing
what I needed to teach was perhaps more
important than Shakespeare or grammar,

guided her hands through the looping,
the pulling of the ends. After several
tries, she got it, walked out the door

empowered. How many lessons are like
that—skills never mastered in childhood,
simple tasks ignored, let go for years?

This morning, my head bald from chemotherapy,
my feet farther away than they used to be
as I bend to my own shoes, that student

returns to teach me the meaning of life:
to simply tie the laces and walk out
of myself into this sunny winter day.

I Am Going to Start Living Like a Mystic

Edward Hirsch

Today I am pulling on a green wool sweater
and walking across the park in a dusky snowfall.

The trees stand like twenty-seven prophets in a field,
each a station in a pilgrimage—silent, pondering.

Blue flakes of light falling across their bodies
are the ciphers of a secret, an occultation.

I will examine their leaves as pages in a text
and consider the bookish pigeons, students of winter.

I will kneel on the track of a vanquished squirrel
and stare into a blank pond for the figure of Sophia.

I shall begin scouring the sky for signs
as if my whole future were constellated upon it.

I will walk home alone with the deep alone,
a disciple of shadows, in praise of the mysteries.

The Uncertainty Principle

Kathleen Norris

for Robert West, O.S.B.

We change it
by looking: what's moving in the heart
or the farthest star,
and when people are true believers
we may know of the mystery
how it works,
or if it does,
but not the two together.

Here at the abbey
bells confide the hour.
A scientist could tell
how crude
a means, how inexact
they are.
Time does not move,
the sky is not blue—the end
of the spectrum
and beginning of light—
it is all in us,
breathed in, let go.

Monks shift in their choir:
stomachs, and the old floor
groan through the homily.
Here in the heart,
where the hours keep,
we are learning eternity
every step of the way.

Now is the Time

Hafiz

Now is the time to know
That all that you do is sacred.

Now, why not consider
A lasting truce with yourself and God.

Now is the time to understand
That all your ideas of right and wrong
Were just a child's training wheels
To be laid aside
When you finally live
With veracity
And love.

Hafiz is a divine envoy
Whom the Beloved
Has written a holy message upon.

My dear, please tell me,
Why do you still
Throw sticks at your heart
And God?

What is it in that sweet voice inside
That incites you to fear?

Now is the time for the world to know
That every thought and action is sacred.

This is the time
For you to deeply compute the impossibility
That there is anything
But Grace.

Now is the season to know
That everything you do
Is sacred.

The Place Where We Are Right

Yehuda Amichai

From the place where we are right
flowers will never grow
in the spring.

The place where we are right
is hard and trampled
like a yard.

But doubts and loves
dig up the world
like a mole, a plow.
And a whisper will be heard in the place
where the ruined
house once stood.

Earthworms

Lynn Ungar

Imagine. The only thing that
God requires of them
is a persistent, wriggling, moving forward,
passing the earth through
the crinkled tube of their bodies
in a motion less like chewing
than like song.

Everything they encounter
goes through them,
as if sunsets, drug store clerks,
diesel fumes and sidewalks
were to move through our very centers
and emerge subtly different
for having fed us—looser somehow,
more open to the possibility of life.

They say the job of angels
is to sing to God in serried choirs.
Perhaps. But most jobs
aren't so glamorous.
Mostly the world depends upon
the silent chanting underneath our feet.
To every grain that enters: "Welcome."
To every parting mote: "Be blessed."

A Poem for My Daughter

Teddy Macker

It seems we have made pain
some kind of mistake,
like having it
is somehow wrong.

Don't let them fool you—
pain is a part of things.

But remember, dear Ellie,
the compost down in the field:
if the rank and dank and dark
are handled well, not merely discarded,
but turned and known and honored,
they one day come to beds of rich earth
home even to the most delicate rose.

~

God comes to you disguised as your life.
Blessings often arrive as trouble.

In French, the word *blesser* means to wound
and relates to the Old English *bletsian*—

to sprinkle with blood.

And in Sanskrit there is a phrase,
a phrase to carry with you
wherever you go:

sarvam annam:

everything is food.

Every last thing.

~

The Navajo people,
it is said,
intentionally wove
(intentionally!)
obvious flaws into their sacred quilts . . .

Why?

It is there, they say,
in the "mistake,"
in the imperfection,

through which the Great Spirit moves.

~

Life is easy, yes.
And life is hard.
Life is simple, yes.
And life is complex.
We are tough, yes. But we are also fragile.
Everything's eternally perfect
but help out if you can.

~

Work on becoming a native of mind, a native of heart.
No thought, no feeling, could ever be "bad."

It's just another creature
in the bestiary of Buddha,
the bestiary of Christ.

Knowing this,
knowing this down to the marrow,
could save you, dear one,
much needless strife.

Remember that wild and strange animals
paused to drink at the pond
of the Buddha's mind
even after he saw
the morning star.

~

No matter what you do, no matter what happens,
it is impossible to leave the path.

Let me say that one more time:
No matter what you do, no matter what happens,
it is impossible to leave the path.

~

Believe it or not, dear Ellie,
some folks carefully imagine
hideous gods tearing at flesh,
clawing at faces,
eating human hearts,
and drinking cups of blood . . .

Why?

To shake hands with the Whole Catastrophe,
to cultivate the Noble Idiot Yes.

According to their tradition,
there are 84,000 "skillful means,"
84,000 tactics of wakefulness,
84,000 ways to become spaciously alive,
84,000 ways to be at home in your life and in this world.

And many of those skillful means are like this one:

enlightenment through endarkment.

~

Life appears to be fundamentally ambiguous.

Wily, everycolored, unpindownable.

For evidence of this, spend time with trees.

Over and over they say,

There is no final word.

And big decisions—
decisions concerning
relationships, concerning children,
concerning death—
are rarely made cleanly.

In general, be wary—
even if just a little—
of talk of purity,
of goodness,
of light.

~

To love everything, not just parts…
To love all of yourself, not just certain traits…
To rest in not knowing…

To carry the cross
and to lay your burden down…

To savor the medicine blue of moon,
the fierce sugar of tangerine…

To be a Christ unto others,
a Christ unto one's self…

To laugh . . .

To be shameless, wild, and silly . . .

To know—fully, headlong,
without compunction—the ordinary magic
of our beautiful human bodies . . .

these seem worthwhile pursuits, life-long tasks.

~

By way of valediction, dear Ellie,
I pass along some words
from our many gracious teachers:

Eden is.

The imperfect is our paradise.

All is grace.

Gracias

Rafael Jesús González

Gracias y benditos sean
el Sol y la Tierra
por este pan y este vino,
        esta fruta, esta carne, esta sal,
        este alimento;
gracias y bendiciones
a quienes lo preparan, lo sirven;
gracias y bendiciones
a quienes lo comparten
(y también a los ausentes y a los difuntos).
Gracias y bendiciones a quienes lo traen
        (que no les falte),
a quienes lo siembran y cultivan,
lo cosechan y lo recogen
        (que no les falte);
gracias y bendiciones a los que trabajan
        y bendiciones a los que no puedan;
que no les falte—su hambre
        hace agrio el vino
        y le roba el gusto a la sal.
Gracias por el sustento y la fuerza
para nuestro bailar y nuestra labor
        por la justicia y la paz.

Grace

Rafael Jesús González

Thanks & blessing be
to the Sun & the Earth
for this bread & this wine,
this fruit, this meat, this salt,
this food;
thanks be & blessing to them
who prepare it, who serve it;
thanks & blessing to them
who share it
(& also the absent & the dead).
Thanks & blessing to them who bring it
(may they not want),
to them who plant & tend it,
harvest & gather it
(may they not want);
thanks & blessing to them who work
& blessing to them who cannot;
may they not want—for their hunger
sours the wine
& robs the salt of its taste.
Thanks be for the sustenance & strength
for our dance & the work of justice, of peace.

Poet's note: I offer this poem in both Spanish and English (two stanzas, if you will). Neither text is a translation of the other. Born and raised on the U.S./Mexico border in El Paso/Ciudad Juárez, I grew up bicultural/bilingual and consequently heir to two muses. My work is almost all discrete pieces in two tongues, and when possible I prefer to publish it as it was written, in both Spanish and English.

Late Fragment

Raymond Carver

And did you get what
you wanted from this life, even so?
I did.
And what did you want?
To call myself beloved, to feel myself
beloved on the earth.

Minobimaadizi

Kimberly Blaeser

On the brow of the weakened world
this August sun still spills warmth.
Here where furrowed hands gather herbs
here in copper memory of *minobimaadizi*,
we camp once more under this canopy of regret,
sprinkle each fragrant offering over fire,
clasp songs tight on throat strings of ancient belonging—
chant belief in any language we know.

Aki. Nibi. Ishkode. Gaye Anishinaabeg.
Nanaandawi'iwe-nagamon.
Sing healing songs for earth that bleeds,
the tired waters, and all the tired warring
peoples. Name the tribes and vibrating cells
of rock and sweetgrass, of tobacco and sage,
of shawl, pipe, drum, and rattle,
of *migizi* wings and sweet cedar-smoke rising.

Here in the strong heart of ceremony
we wait, leaves and *noodin* teaching a spiral calm.
Soon words gather like medicine—
mashkiki, beaded now into seeded images,
into litanies of clan relatives: loon songs
and bear stories, the mineral regalia of sky.
Once more echoes of crane calls nourish our journey,
rhythm lifting the sad fever of forgetfulness.

Everywhere making us whole. *Mino-ayaa.*

For a brief note regarding the cultural context of this poem, see Notes on the Poems.

Zazen on Ching-t'ing Mountain

Li Po

The birds have vanished down the sky.
Now the last cloud drains away.

We sit together, the mountain and me,
until only the mountain remains.

You Are There

Erica Jong

You are there.
You have always been
there.
Even when you thought
you were climbing
you had already arrived.
Even when you were
breathing hard,
you were at rest.
Even then it was clear
you were there.

Not in our nature
to know what
is journey and what
arrival.
Even if we knew
we would not admit.
Even if we lived
we would think
we were just
germinating.

To live is to be
uncertain.
Certainty comes
at the end.

Learning from Trees

Grace Butcher

If we could,
like the trees,
practice dying,
do it every year
just as something we do—
like going on vacation
or celebrating birthdays—
it would become
as easy a part of us
as our hair or clothing.

Someone would show us how
to lie down and fade away
as if in deepest meditation,
and we would learn
about the fine dark emptiness,
both knowing it and not knowing it,
and coming back would be irrelevant.

Whatever it is the trees know
when they stand undone,
surprisingly intricate,
we need to know also
so we can allow
that last thing
to happen to us
as if it were only
any ordinary thing,

leaves and lives
falling away, the spirit, complex,
waiting in the fine darkness
to learn which way
it will go.

Savasana: Corpse Pose

Marianne Murphy Zarzana

On the bonsai-green carpet, you stretch
your frame out flat upon a blue yoga mat,

and parallel, I lie down upon a purple one,
both of us becoming still, our bodies sinking

further into the floor with each slow, steady
breath. It's night, and together we're letting go.

Mollie, our old black lab mix, wanders in, licks
your open palm, sniffs my hair, snuffles, settles

by my head with labored breath. Soon, I know,
we'll lose her. Someday, each other. This is

practice. We're learning to dissolve, surrender
to earth, release thighs, hips, neck, skull, all

the bones, pay attention only to breath—let it
become a ribbon, the texture of fine silk.

Surprised by Evening

Robert Bly

There is unknown dust that is near us,
Waves breaking on shores just over the hill,
Trees full of birds that we have never seen,
Nets drawn down with dark fish.

The evening arrives; we look up and it is there,
It has come through the nets of the stars,
Through the tissues of the grass,
Walking quietly over the asylums of the waters.

The day shall never end, we think:
We have hair that seems born for the daylight;
But, at last, the quiet waters of the night will rise,
And our skin shall see far off, as it does under water.

Rain on Water

Freya Manfred

All afternoon rain streams down on the lake
until a break in the black clouds
draws me out of the house
into the rocking waves.

I dive through layers of darkness, layers of light,
and when I come up for air,
the sky echoes the underwater world,
speaking the unspoken,

not a warning, or god-like, "It shall be!"—
more a wind-driven, earth-embracing, *word*—
and I swim to meet it,
from the lake into the sky.

Next to this the body is nothing,
and the mind less than the body,
and only the country of the heart
is equal to what I know.

Trough

Judy Sorum Brown

There is a trough in waves,
A low spot
Where horizon disappears
And only sky
And water
Are our company.
And there we lose our way
Unless
We rest, knowing the wave will bring us
To its crest again.
There we may drown
If we let fear
Hold us within its grip and shake us
Side to side,
And leave us flailing, torn, disoriented.

But if we rest there
In the trough,
Are silent,
Being with
The low part of the wave,
Keeping
Our energy and
Noticing the shape of things,
The flow,

Then time alone
Will bring us to another
Place
Where we can see
Horizon, see the land again,
Regain our sense
Of where
We are,
And where we need to swim.

One's Ship Comes In

Joe Paddock

I swear
my way now will be
to continue without
plan or hope, to accept
the drift of things, to shift
from endless effort
to joy in, say,
that robin, plunging
into the mossy shallows
of my bird bath and
splashing madly till
the air shines with spray.
Joy it will be, say,
in Nancy, pretty in pink
and rumpled T-shirt,
rubbing sleep from her eyes, or
joy even in
just this breathing, free
of fright and clutch, knowing
how one's ship comes in
with each such breath.

Then too there is this

J. Allyn Rosser

joy in the day's being done, however
clumsily, and in the ticked-off lists,
the packages nestling together,
no one home waiting for dinner, for
you, no one impatient for your touch
or kind words to salve what nightly
rises like heartburn, the ghost-lump feeling
that one is really as alone as one had feared.
One isn't, not really. Not really. Joy
to see over the strip mall, darkening
right on schedule, a neon-proof pink
sunset flaring like the roof of a cat's mouth,
cleanly ribbed, the clouds laddering up
and lit as if by a match struck somewhere
in the throat much deeper down.

Ich liebe meines Wesens Dunkelstunden (I love the dark hours of my being)

Rainer Maria Rilke

I love the dark hours of my being.
My mind deepens into them.
There I can find, as in old letters,
the days of my life, already lived,
and held like a legend, and understood.

Then the knowing comes: I can open
to another life that's wide and timeless.

So I am sometimes like a tree
rustling over a gravesite
and making real the dream
of the one its living roots
embrace:

a dream once lost
among sorrows and songs.

Burning the Journals

Robyn Sarah

The past is useless
to me now:
an old suitcase
with mould in the lining,
heavy even when empty—

heavy empty,
like the bronze bell
of the Russian church,
clapperless
in the grass;

so I shall have to go
on from here with less
to bank on. My peeled eye.
The way things sing
in the sun.

Flowering

Linda Buckmaster

At the Ruins of the Seven Churches, Inishmore

Pick a crevice
a homey gap
between stones
and make it
your own.

Grow a life here
from wind, rain,
and the memories
of ancients embedded
in limestone.

The bees will use you
for their sweet honey.
The rock will soften
under your touch. You will
draw moisture from fog
and hold it. Your presence
will build soil.

This is all we have
in this life, all we own:
a flowering
an opening
a gap between stones
for tiny tender roots.

The Moment

Margaret Atwood

The moment when, after many years
of hard work and a long voyage
you stand in the centre of your room,
house, half-acre, square mile, island, country,
knowing at last how you got there,
and say, *I own this*,

is the same moment when the trees unloose
their soft arms from around you,
the birds take back their language,
the cliffs fissure and collapse,
the air moves back from you like a wave
and you can't breathe.

No, they whisper. *You own nothing.*
You were a visitor, time after time
climbing the hill, planting the flag, proclaiming.
We never belonged to you.
You never found us.
It was always the other way round.

Wakarusa Medicine Wheel

Denise Low

The hearth in the middle smolders. Cedar limbs spark lava-red.

To the East stands a limestone marker tilted to equinox sunrise. Offerings cover the grainy surface—red-cloth tobacco ties, brass keys, eagle fluff, a silver dollar.

To the West another stelae marks end of day, finish of the sun's round.

A stone to the North is covered with glistening quartz shards, quills, a bear claw, and pine.

Gifts to the Southern marker are robin feathers, buffalo nickels, seed corn, an obsidian arrowhead.

Smoke drifts east, where a thunderbird stretches. Bluestem grass ripples in its earthbound wings.

Sparrows roost in a nearby jack oak. A night hawk calls.

For a brief note regarding the cultural context of this poem, see Notes on the Poems.

Rankin Ridge

Linda M. Hasselstrom

The sun drops below the high tree.
Elk cows the color of grass move
out of the pines,
up the meadows toward a pond.
Dark among the trees the bulls pace,
snort, begin to bugle.
That sound flows across meadows like water,
opening like a piccolo, rising to a keen,
a cry, a wail, a ululation for the night.

The moon lifts,
huge, gold, flattened,
pushing to higher air,
becoming small, silver, distant.

The cows graze, silent in the glowing grass.
The bulls wait at the edge of the trees,
bugling still.
The moonlight flickers
at sounds too high for human ears.

Listening Deeply

Dick Allen

Listening deeply,
sometimes—in another—you can hear
the sound of a hermit, sighing
as he climbs a mountain trail to reach a waterfall
or a Buddhist nun reciting prayers
while moonlight falls through the window onto an old clay floor,
and once in a while you find a child
rolling a hoop through the alleyways of Tokyo, laughing,
or a farmer pausing in a rice field to watch geese fly,
the thoughts on his lips he doesn't think to say.

Soundings

Joyce Sutphen

In the afternoon of summer, sounds
come through the window: a tractor
muttering to itself as it

pivots at the corner of the
hay field, stalled for a moment
as the green row feeds into the baler.

The wind slips a whisper behind
an ear; the noise of the highway
is like the dark green stem of a rose.

From the kitchen the blunt banging
of cupboard doors and wooden chairs
makes a lonely echo in the floor.

Somewhere, between the breeze
and the faraway sound of a train,
comes a line of birdsong, lightly
threading the heavy cloth of dream.

the door

Miroslav Holub

Go and open the door.
  Maybe outside there's
    a tree, or a wood,
    a garden,
    or a magic city.

Go and open the door.
    Maybe a dog's rummaging.
    Maybe you'll see a face,
or an eye,
or the picture
        of a picture.

Go and open the door.
    If there's a fog
    it will clear.

Go and open the door.
    Even if there's only
    the darkness ticking,
    even if there's only
    the hollow wind,
    even if
      nothing
          is there,
go and open the door.

At least
there'll be
a draught.

Meeting the Light Completely

Jane Hirshfield

Even the long-beloved
was once
an unrecognized stranger.

Just so,
the chipped lip
of a blue-glazed cup,
blown field
of a yellow curtain,
might also,
flooding and falling,
ruin your heart.

A table painted with roses.
An empty clothesline.

Each time,
the found world surprises—
that is its nature.

And then
what is said by all lovers:
"What fools we were, not to have seen."

Rutabaga

Laura Grace Weldon

You darken as my knife slices,
blushing at what you become.
I save your thick leaves,
your purple skin
to feed the cows.

A peasant guest at any meal,
you agree to hide in fragrant stew
or gleam nakedly
in butter and chives.

Though your seeds are tiny
you grow with fierce will,
grateful for poor soil and dry days,
heave up from the ground
under sheltering stalks
and wait to sweeten with the frost.

Tonight we take you into our bodies
as if we do you a favor,
letting your molecules
become a higher being,
one that knows music and art.

But you share with us
what makes you a rutabaga.
Through you we eat sunlight,
taste the soil's clamoring mysteries,
gain your seed's perfect might.

Think of Others

Mahmoud Darwish

As you prepare your breakfast, think of others
    (do not forget the pigeon's food).
As you conduct your wars, think of others
    (do not forget those who seek peace).
As you pay your water bill, think of others
    (those who are nursed by clouds).
As you return home, to your home, think of others
    (do not forget the people of the camps).
As you sleep and count the stars, think of others
    (those who have nowhere to sleep).
As you express yourself in metaphor, think of others
    (those who have lost the right to speak).
As you think of others far away, think of yourself
    (say: *If only I were a candle in the dark*).

Twilight

Louise Glück

All day he works at his cousin's mill,
so when he gets home at night, he always sits at this one window,
sees one time of day, twilight.
There should be more time like this, to sit and dream.
It's as his cousin says:
Living—living takes you away from sitting.

In the window, not the world but a squared-off landscape
representing the world. The seasons change,
each visible only a few hours a day.
Green things followed by golden things followed by whiteness—
abstractions from which come intense pleasures,
like the figs on the table.

At dusk, the sun goes down in a haze of red fire between two poplars.
It goes down late in summer—sometimes it's hard to stay awake.

Then everything falls away.
The world for a little longer
is something to see, then only something to hear,
crickets, cicadas.
Or to smell sometimes, aroma of lemon trees, of orange trees.
Then sleep takes this away also.

But it's easy to give things up like this, experimentally,
for a matter of hours.

I open my fingers—
I let everything go.

Visual world, language,
rustling of leaves in the night,
smell of high grass, of woodsmoke.

I let it go, then I light the candle.

Instructions for the Journey

Pat Schneider

The self you leave behind
is only a skin you have outgrown.
Don't grieve for it.
Look to the wet, raw, unfinished
self, the one you are becoming.
The world, too, sheds its skin:
politicians, cataclysms, ordinary days.
It's easy to lose this tenderly
unfolding moment. Look for it
as if it were the first green blade
after a long winter. Listen for it
as if it were the first clear tone
in a place where dawn is heralded by bells.

And if all that fails,
wash your own dishes.
Rinse them.
Stand in your kitchen at your sink.
Let cold water run between your fingers.
Feel it.

Plate

Al Zolynas

I receive only to give away.
My life is simple
and full of surrender:
I'm picked up, put down.
In the end, I'm always made clean
or broken.

I Will Keep Broken Things

Alice Walker

I will keep
broken
things:
The big clay
pot
with raised
iguanas
chasing
their
tails;
two
of their
wise
heads
sheared
off;

I will keep
broken
things:
The old
slave
market
basket
brought
to my
door
by Mississippi
a jagged
hole
gouged
in its sturdy
dark
oak
side.

I will keep
broken
things:
The memory
of
those
long
delicious
night
swims
with
you;

I will keep
broken
things:
In my house
there
remains
an
honored
shelf
on which
I will
keep
broken
things.

Their beauty
is
they
need
not
ever
be
"fixed."

I will keep
your
wild
free
laughter
though
it is now
missing
its
reassuring
and

graceful
hinge.

I will keep
broken
things:

*Thank you
so much!*

I will keep
broken
things.
I will keep
you:

pilgrim
of
sorrow.

I will keep
myself.

The Way It Is

Rosemerry Wahtola Trommer

Over and over we break
open, we break and
we break and we open.
For a while, we try to fix
the vessel—as if
to be broken is bad.
As if with glue and tape
and a steady hand we
might bring things to perfect
again. As if they were ever
perfect. As if to be broken is not
also perfect. As if to be open
is not the path toward joy.

The vase that's been shattered
and cracked will never
hold water. Eventually
it will leak. And at some
point, perhaps, we decide
that we're done with picking
our flowers anyway, and no
longer need a place to contain them
We watch them grow just
as wildflowers do—unfenced,
unmanaged, blossoming only
when they're ready—and mygod,
how beautiful they are amidst
the mounting pile of shards.

The Bright Field

R. S. Thomas

I have seen the sun break through
to illuminate a small field
for a while, and gone my way
and forgotten it. But that was the pearl
of great price, the one field that had
the treasure in it. I realize now
that I must give all that I have
to possess it. Life is not hurrying

on to a receding future, nor hankering after
an imagined past. It is the turning
aside like Moses to the miracle
of the lit bush, to a brightness
that seemed as transitory as your youth
once, but is the eternity that awaits you.

The Good News

Thich Nhat Hanh

The good news
they do not print.
The good news
we do print.
We have a special edition every moment,
and we need you to read it.
The good news is that you are alive,
that the linden tree is still there,
standing firm in the harsh winter.
The good news is that you have wonderful eyes
to touch the blue sky.
The good news is that your child is there before you,
and your arms are available:
hugging is possible.
They only print what is wrong.
Look at each of our special editions.
We always offer the things that are not wrong.
We want you to benefit from them
and help protect them.
The dandelion is there by the sidewalk,
smiling its wondrous smile,
singing the song of eternity.
Listen. You have ears that can hear it.
Bow your head.
Listen to it.
Leave behind the world of sorrow,
of preoccupation,
and get free.
The latest good news
is that you can do it.

Sweet Darkness

David Whyte

When your eyes are tired
the world is tired also.

When your vision has gone
no part of the world can find you.

Time to go into the dark
where the night has eyes
to recognize its own.

There you can be sure
you are not beyond love.

The dark will be your womb
tonight.

The night will give you a horizon
further than you can see.

You must learn one thing.
The world was made to be free in.

Give up all the other worlds
except the one to which you belong.

Sometimes it takes darkness and the sweet
confinement of your aloneness
to learn

anything or anyone
that does not bring you alive

is too small for you.

For the Sake of Strangers

Dorianne Laux

No matter what the grief, its weight,
we are obliged to carry it.
We rise and gather momentum, the dull strength
that pushes us through crowds.
And then the young boy gives me directions
so avidly. A woman holds the glass door open,
waiting patiently for my empty body to pass through.
All day it continues, each kindness
reaching toward another—a stranger
singing to no one as I pass on the path, trees
offering their blossoms, a child
who lifts his almond eyes and smiles.
Somehow they always find me, seem even
to be waiting, determined to keep me
from myself, from the thing that calls to me
as it must have once called to them—
this temptation to step off the edge
and fall weightless, away from the world.

The Thing Is

Ellen Bass

to love life, to love it even
when you have no stomach for it
and everything you've held dear
crumbles like burnt paper in your hands,
your throat filled with the silt of it.
When grief sits with you, its tropical heat
thickening the air, heavy as water
more fit for gills than lungs;
when grief weights you like your own flesh
only more of it, an obesity of grief,
you think, *How can a body withstand this?*
Then you hold life like a face
between your palms, a plain face,
no charming smile, no violet eyes,
and you say, yes, I will take you
I will love you, again.

The Cure

Albert Huffstickler

We think we get over things.
We don't get over things.
Or say, we get over the measles
but not a broken heart.
We need to make that distinction.
The things that become part of our experience
never become less a part of our experience.
How can I say it?
The way to "get over" a life is to die.
Short of that, you move with it,
let the pain be pain,
not in the hope that it will vanish
but in the faith that it will fit in,
find its place in the shape of things
and be then not any less pain but true to form.
Because anything natural has an inherent shape
and will flow towards it.
And a life is as natural as a leaf.
That's what we're looking for:
not the end of a thing but the shape of it.
Wisdom is seeing the shape of your life
without obliterating (getting over) a single
instant of it.

Consider the Space Between Stars

Linda Pastan

Consider the white space
between words on a page, not just
the margins around them.

Or the space between thoughts:
instants when the mind is inventing
exactly what it thinks

and the mouth waits
to be filled with language.
Consider the space

between lovers after a quarrel,
the white sheet a cold metaphor
between them.

Now picture the brief space
before death enters, hat in hand:
vanishing years, filled with light.

Winter Grace

Patricia Fargnoli

If you have seen the snow
under the lamppost
piled up like a white beaver hat on the picnic table
or somewhere slowly falling
into the brook
to be swallowed by water,
then you have seen beauty
and known it for its transience.
And if you have gone out in the snow
for only the pleasure
of walking barely protected
from the galaxies,
the flakes settling on your parka
like the dust from just-born stars,
the cold waking you
as if from long sleeping,
then you can understand
how, more often than not,
truth is found in silence,
how the natural world comes to you
if you go out to meet it,
its icy ditches filled with dead weeds,
its vacant birdhouses, and dens
full of the sleeping.
But this is the slowed down season
held fast by darkness
and if no one comes to keep you company
then keep watch over your own solitude.
In that stillness, you will learn
with your whole body
the significance of the cold
and the night,
which is otherwise always eluding you.

Solstice

Robyn Sarah

A sly gift it is, that on the year's
shortest day, the sun
stays longest in this house—

extends the wand of its slow
slant and distant squint
farthest into the long depths

of our wintry rooms—to touch, with
tremulous light, interior places
it has not lit before.

My Father at the Piano

Mary O'Connor

When he still had the Bechstein he turned the seat and instrument
to the French windows, so if he looked up in reverie he saw the garden,
grass springing through crazy-paving meant to suppress it, where roses
survived and sometimes sweet pea climbed the opposing fence,
and up the rise a disused railway line became a path for hikers.

But I think his reverie was always with the music: notes and values,
composer's markings, meaning found in minims and semibreves spoken
by his soft unworkmanlike hands. He could be carried off, taken away,
transported outside himself—his tentative, make-do self, his failed
marriage, broken family, and later this life with an ailing mother—

into a paradise of logic and beauty untouched by foibles or decay.
The Bechstein had a soft tone and easy action; his dad had bought it
second-hand in the twenties, already mellowed by generations,
so now a light touch made a velvet *pianissimo*, and children
perched there for lessons felt in their small hands power enough.

The time he spent with it! Meticulous, joyful work, dissecting problems,
attending to the technical: tone, dynamics, color, phrasing. I saw
this was practice, absorbing the whole being, mind, heart, limbs.
Forgetting self in pursuit of the real, the incorruptible. Which
was not to say perfection, but readiness. To receive the something,

to be there the moment the something happened.

Parallel the Care the Dancer Takes

Hafiz

Parallel the care the dancer takes on her
finest step.

You need to feel the craving for that
unison, you need to know all the
longing the great ones had to suffer

before God said to them, *"Here I am,
yours to do with whatever you like."*

And when will the Beloved say such
a sublime thing to you, give you all that
power?

A prerequisite is: when all you touch,
you touch as if it were sacred.

That will bring your mind to a standstill.
The space between you and any object

will then open up into a sea of radiance,
where you can drown for a second, drown,
and taste me.

Another Ocean

Ruby R. Wilson

after Mary Oliver

I read her poems
about the sea

and wish that I lived near one
until I remember

the wind that weaves
soil, grass, and sky

the design of fox and pheasant
tracks in the snow

and the owl I hear
at night who

leaves fierce signs
of its hunting nearby

and my silent
ski trail that the wind

erases through the prairie
from which I came.

Entrance

Rainer Maria Rilke

Whoever you are: step out of doors tonight,
Out of the room that lets you feel secure.
Infinity is open to your sight.
Whoever you are.
With eyes that have forgotten how to see
From viewing things already too well-known,
Lift up into the dark a huge, black tree
And put it in the heavens: tall, alone.
And you have made the world and all you see.
It ripens like the words still in your mouth.
And when at last you comprehend its truth,
Then close your eyes and gently set it free.

Saying Our Names

Marianne Murphy Zarzana

for Judi Brown

Notice how just one syllable—
say *Jack*—can expand and become
the world, round and whole,
when it is a child's name
being formed by a mother's mouth.

I've overheard women in stores and airports,
restaurants and trains, sprinkling their talk
with the name of a brand new baby or
a grown child—*Morgen, Nora,*
Michael, Kyle, Joseph, Ava-Rose.

They sing each vowel and consonant
so the name stands out, resonates,
a pure bell, whether the tone struck
is a major key, proud and strong,
or a diminished minor note.

Sometimes, when my daughter catches
her own name, *Elaine May*, part of a story
I am telling a sister over the phone,
later she'll ask, quasi-annoyed,
were you talking about me?

Yes, endlessly, shamelessly, I tell stories
about you. I say those fluid syllables,
chosen for the meaning—*light*—
and to honor your grandmothers,
chosen after discarding countless names.

Yes, I say them again and again and wonder
at the world they have become. Is this
how God says our names? Is this why sometimes
when I hear the wind rustling through the trees,
I turn and listen?

Walking a Field into Evening

Larry Smith

For learned books, I read the grasses.
For reputation, a bird calls my name.
I cross a stone bridge with the pace of dusk.
At the meadow gate, six cows meditate.

For decades I ran my mind up hill and down;
now idleness tells me what is near.
An arrow of wild geese crosses the sky,
my body still, my feet firm on the ground.

We age like trees now, watch our seedlings
take wind or grow around us.
I'm going to mark my books lightly
with a pencil. When someone wants
to take my picture, I'll walk towards them
and embrace.

                    No more arguments,
just heart sense, or talk about nothing.
Take long walks in the woods at dawn and dusk,
breathe in the damp musty air,
learn to listen before I die.

Sometimes, I Am Startled Out of Myself,

Barbara Crooker

like this morning, when the wild geese came squawking,
flapping their rusty hinges, and something about their trek
across the sky made me think about my life, the places
of brokenness, the places of sorrow, the places where grief
has strung me out to dry. And then the geese come calling,
the leader falling back when tired, another taking her place.
Hope is borne on wings. Look at the trees. They turn to gold
for a brief while, then lose it all each November.
Through the cold months, they stand, take the worst
weather has to offer. And still, they put out shy green leaves
come April, come May. The geese glide over the cornfields,
land on the pond with its sedges and reeds.
You do not have to be wise. Even a goose knows how to find
shelter, where the corn still lies in the stubble and dried stalks.
All we do is pass through here, the best way we can.
They stitch up the sky, and it is whole again.

Blue Herons

Twyla M. Hansen

What does it mean—all day
rain coming straight down, slow,
a noticeable absence of wind,
leaves plush beneath canopies,
stilt-legs in the flooded fields?

All morning I have glimpsed them—
along this highway bottomland
the river tried hard to reclaim,
broken dikes and debris and backwater—
blue-gray sentinels nearly motionless,
patient for a meal.

And what can we do—
in these wide-open spaces
where mud creeks are capable
of churning out of their banks,
flattening brome and fence and farmland—

but to take inventory of threatened senses,
to pick ourselves up above the water,
to rise, to rise?

No Fishing

David Allan Evans

I was sprawled out on
my belly in a rowboat,
watching the green
lake of my face.

When I reached and felt
the cold water,
my hands, cut off at
the wrists,

flew into the
sky with two gulls.

Wooden Boats

Judy Sorum Brown

I have a brother who builds wooden boats,
Who knows precisely how a board
Can bend or turn, steamed just exactly
Soft enough so he, with help of friends,
Can shape it to the hull.

The knowledge lies as much
Within his sure hands on the plane
As in his head;
It lies in love of wood and grain,
A rough hand resting on the satin
Of the finished deck.

Is there within us each
Such artistry forgotten
In the cruder tasks
The world requires of us,
The faster modern work
That we have
Turned our life to do?

Could we return to more of craft
Within our lives,
And feel the way the grain of wood runs true,
By letting our hands linger
On the product of our artistry?
Could we recall what we have known
But have forgotten,
The gifts within ourselves,
Each other too,
And thus transform a world
As he and friends do,
Shaping steaming oak boards
Upon the hulls of wooden boats?

Putting in a Window

John Brantingham

Carpentry has a rhythm that should never
be violated. You need to move slowly,
methodically, never trying to finish early,
never hoping that you'd be done sooner.
It's best if you work without thought of the
end. If hurried, you end up with crooked
door joints and drafty rooms. Do not work
after you are annoyed just so the job
will be done more quickly. Stop when you
begin to curse at the wood. Putting in
a window should be a joy. You should love
the new header and the sound of
your electric screwdriver as it secures
the new beams. The only good carpenter
is the one who knows that he's not good.
He's afraid that he'll ruin the whole house,
and works slowly. It's the same as
cooking or driving. The good cook
knows humility, and his soufflé never falls
because he is terrified that it will fall
the whole time he's cooking. The good driver
knows that he might plow into a mother
walking her three-year old, and so watches
for them carefully. The good carpenter
knows that his beams might be weak, and a misstep
might ruin the place he loves. In the end,
you find your own pace, and you lose time.
When you started, the sun was high. Now
that you're finished, it's dark. Tomorrow, you
might put in a door. The next day,
you'll start on your new deck.

Moon

Billy Collins

The moon is full tonight
an illustration for sheet music,
an image in Matthew Arnold
glimmering on the English Channel,
or a ghost over a smoldering battlefield
in one of the history plays.

It's as full as it was
in that poem by Coleridge
where he carries his year-old son
into the orchard behind the cottage
and turns the baby's face to the sky
to see for the first time
the earth's bright companion,
something amazing to make his crying seem small.

And if you wanted to follow this example,
tonight would be the night
to carry some tiny creature outside
and introduce him to the moon.

And if your house has no child,
you can always gather into your arms
the sleeping infant of yourself,
as I have done tonight,
and carry him outdoors,
all limp in his tattered blanket,
making sure to steady his lolling head
with the palm of your hand.

And while the wind ruffles the pear trees
in the corner of the orchard
and dark roses wave against a stone wall,
you can turn him on your shoulder
and walk in circles on the lawn
drunk with the light.
You can lift him up into the sky,
your eyes nearly as wide as his,
as the moon climbs high into the night.

The Last Things I'll Remember

Joyce Sutphen

The partly open hay barn door, white frame around the darkness,
the broken board, small enough for a child
to slip through.

Walking in the cornfields in late July, green tassels overhead,
the slap of flat leaves as we pass, silent
and invisible from any road.

Hollyhocks leaning against the stucco house, peonies heavy
as fruit, drooping their deep heads
on the dog house roof.

Lilac bushes between the lawn and the woods,
a tractor shifting from one gear into
the next, the throttle opened,

the smell of cut hay, rain coming across the river,
the drone of the hammer mill,
milk-machines at dawn.

When I Am Wise

Mary Gray

When I am wise in the speech of grass,
I forget the sound of words
and walk into the bottomland
and lie with my head on the ground
and listen to what grass tells me
about small places for wind to sing,
about the labor of insects,
about shadows dank with spice,
and the friendliness of weeds.

When I am wise in the dance of grass,
I forget the name and run
into the rippling bottomland
and lean against the silence which flows
out of the crumpled mountains
and rises through slick blades, pods,
wheat stems, and curly shoots,
and is carried by wind for miles
from my outstretched hands.

Trees

Howard Nemerov

To be a giant and keep quiet about it,
To stay in one's own place;
To stand for the constant presence of process
And always to seem the same;
To be steady as a rock and always trembling,
Having the hard appearance of death
With the soft, fluent nature of growth,
One's Being deceptively armored,
One's Becoming deceptively vulnerable;
To be so tough, and take the light so well,
Freely providing forbidden knowledge
Of so many things about heaven and earth
For which we should otherwise have no word—
Poems or people are rarely so lovely,
And even when they have great qualities
They tend to tell you rather than exemplify
What they believe themselves to be about,
While from the moving silence of trees,
Whether in storm or calm, in leaf and naked,
Night and day, we draw conclusions of our own,
Sustaining and unnoticed as our breath
And perilous also—though there has never been
A critical tree—about the nature of things.

Moth Koan

Richard Schiffman

You say that you are troubled
by your own thoughts. Listen,
even the moth casts a shadow
when it flies before the sun.
Do you think the sun is troubled,
or the ground, or the moth,
for that matter? No, what is
troubled is the shadow thinking
it's the moth that has fallen
to the ground, where the sun
will never shine again. The moth
that understands this
flies straight to the sun.

At the Teahouse, 6 am

Holly J. Hughes

Sunrise at the octagonal hut;
beyond, where two decks meet,
a lizard does pushups in the sun.
I see the green, chattering world
through the window, I see
my image in the window.
Both are present; are both true?
A bee enters the hut, buzzes
insistently against the window,
but the window won't yield
to his wishes. I want to
show him the open door,
say *this world through the glass*
is only an illusion but I don't.
How long will he hurl himself
against the dusty glass? How long
will we believe we are not free?

In Plowboy's Produce Market

Donna Hilbert

I push my cart through Plowboy's produce market,
gleaning this song for the first days of fall:

broccoli cauliflower cabbage kohlrabi

The price of red pepper is dropping.
Eggplant shines purple,
bell pepper green.

I watch an old couple choose string beans:
She fills their sack by handfuls. He frowns,
empties it back into the bin,
fills it again, turning each bean to the light
before dropping it in.

pattypan crook-neck pumpkin zucchini

A woman wearing a scarf tight at her chin
eats Thompson's seedless from the grape bin.

Tokay Exotic Muscat Red Flame

At the melons, a man in white shorts, skin brown
as russet potatoes, swings a cantaloupe into his cart.
I think I'm in love.

Winesap Pippin Golden Delicious

This week, apples.
Last week, plums.

Old man, kiss your wife.
Wash your face in the juice of ripe fruit.
Put beans into your sack without looking.
Every bean is perfect, every bean is right.

The Moment

Marie Howe

Oh, the coming-out-of-nowhere moment

when,   nothing

happens

no what-have-I-to-do-today-list

maybe   half a moment

the rush of traffic stops.

The whir of I should be, I should be, I should be

slows to silence,

the white cotton curtains hanging still.

Fog

Twyla M. Hansen

The fog comes as a surprise, forms in silence
overnight, so when you part the curtain
a white blur muffles the known world.

Moving through, no escape, every last
green leaf dotted silver, last night's
moisture glistens on grass tips,

until you cross the footbridge and stop:
below is a world most will miss,
vehicles in a rush to somewhere else.

Fifty yards down the creek a heron
poises in shallow water perfectly still,
grassy banks lined with tracks of deer.

On the far side a dozen wild turkeys
cross a mowed clearing, one by one,
to fence line and then to field, to forage,

and overhead, in this ground-cloud,
Canada geese come in for a landing
you can hear but not yet see,

because this old planet still has a few tricks
in its bag, a monkey wrench or two to make
us pay attention, to slow down, as drivers

do, the whine of tires on pavement muted.
As you turn back, the fog clears. Yet
all day you will hold this other world close.

No More Same Old Silly Love Songs

Neil Carpathios

When the radio in my car broke I started to notice the trees.
I began to stop exaggerating the color of leaves,
how their reds and oranges need no wordy embellishment.
I started to open my window and smell the wet pavement
after morning rain. Crows on the phone line,
their blackness and stubborn dignity. I even noticed my hands
gripping the wheel, the small dark hairs, the skin,
the knuckles and the perfect blue veins.

An Observation

May Sarton

True gardeners cannot bear a glove
Between the sure touch and the tender root,
Must let their hands grow knotted as they move
With a rough sensitivity about
Under the earth, between the rock and shoot,
Never to bruise or wound the hidden fruit.
And so I watched my mother's hands grow scarred,
She who could heal the wounded plant or friend
With the same vulnerable yet rigorous love;
I minded once to see her beauty gnarled,
But now her truth is given me to live,
As I learn for myself we must be hard
To move among the tender with an open hand,
And to stay sensitive up to the end
Pay with some toughness for a gentle world.

Wage Peace

Judyth Hill

Wage peace with your breath.

Breathe in firemen and rubble,
breathe out whole buildings and flocks of red wing blackbirds.

Breathe in terrorists
and breathe out sleeping children and freshly mown fields.

Breathe in confusion and breathe out maple trees.

Breathe in the fallen and breathe out lifelong friendships intact.

Wage peace with your listening: hearing sirens, pray loud.

Remember your tools: flower seeds, clothes pins, clean rivers.

Make soup.

Play music, memorize the words for thank you in three languages.

Learn to knit, and make a hat.

Think of chaos as dancing raspberries,
imagine grief
as the outbreath of beauty
or the gesture of fish.

Swim for the other side.

Wage peace.

Never has the world seemed so fresh and precious:

Have a cup of tea … and rejoice.

Act as if armistice has already arrived.
Celebrate today.

What Else

Carolyn Locke

The way the trees empty themselves of leaves,
let drop their ponderous fruit,
the way the turtle abandons the sun-warmed log,
the way even the late-blooming aster
succumbs to the power of frost—

this is not a new story.
Still, on this morning, the hollowness
of the season startles, filling
the rooms of your house, filling the world
with impossible light, improbable hope.

And so, what else can you do
but let yourself be broken
and emptied? What else is there
but waiting in the autumn sun?

On Pain

Kahlil Gibran

And a woman spoke, saying, Tell us of Pain.
And he said:
Your pain is the breaking of the shell that encloses
 your understanding.
Even as the stone of the fruit must break, that its
 heart may stand in the sun, so must you know
 pain.
And could you keep your heart in wonder at the daily
 miracles of your life, your pain would not seem
 less wondrous than your joy;
And you would accept the seasons of your heart,
 even as you have always accepted the seasons
 that pass over your fields.
And you would watch with serenity through the
 winters of your grief.

Much of your pain is self-chosen.
It is the bitter potion by which the physician within
 you heals your sick self.
Therefore trust the physician, and drink his remedy
 in silence and tranquility:
For his hand, though heavy and hard, is guided by
 the tender hand of the Unseen,
And the cup he brings, though it burn your lips, has
 been fashioned of the clay which the Potter has
 moistened with His own sacred tears.

The Joins

Chana Bloch

> Kintsugi *is the Japanese art of mending precious pottery with gold.*

What's between us
seems flexible as the webbing
between forefinger and thumb.

Seems flexible but isn't;
what's between us
is made of clay

like any cup on the shelf.
It shatters easily. Repair
becomes the task.

We glue the wounded edges
with tentative fingers.
Scar tissue is visible history

and the cup is precious to us
because
we saved it.

In the art of *kintsugi*
a potter repairing a broken cup
would sprinkle the resin

with powdered gold.
Sometimes the joins
are so exquisite

they say the potter
may have broken the cup
just so he could mend it.

Companion for Life

Hafiz

Our union is like this: If you feel cold I would
reach for a blanket to cover *our* shivering feet.

If a hunger comes into your body I would run
to my garden and start digging potatoes.

If you asked for a few words of comfort and
guidance I would quickly kneel by your side
and offer you a whole book … as a gift.

If you ever ache with loneliness so much
you weep, I would say,

*Here is a rope, tie it around me, Hafiz will be
your companion for life.*

Bedside Manners

Christopher Wiseman

How little the dying seem to need—
A drink perhaps, a little food,
A smile, a hand to hold, medication,
A change of clothes, an unspoken
Understanding about what's happening.
You think it would be more, much more,
Something more difficult for us
To help with in this great disruption,
But perhaps it's because as the huge shape
Rears up higher and darker each hour
They are anxious that we should see it too
And try to show us with a hand-squeeze.

We panic to do more for them,
And especially when it's your father,
And his eyes are far away, and your tears
Are all down your face and clothes,
And he doesn't see them now, but smiles
Perhaps, just perhaps, because you're there.
How little he needs. Just love. More Love.

To Have Without Holding

Marge Piercy

Learning to love differently is hard,
love with the hands wide open, love
with the doors banging on their hinges,
the cupboard unlocked, the wind
roaring and whimpering in the rooms
rustling the sheets and snapping the blinds
that thwack like rubber bands
in an open palm.

It hurts to love wide open
stretching the muscles that feel
as if they are made of wet plaster,
then of blunt knives, then
of sharp knives.

It hurts to thwart the reflexes
of grab, of clutch; to love and let
go again and again. It pesters to remember
the lover who is not in the bed,
to hold back what is owed to the work
that gutters like a candle in a cave
without air, to love consciously,
conscientiously, concretely, constructively.

I can't do it, you say it's killing
me, but you thrive, you glow
on the street like a neon raspberry,
You float and sail, a helium balloon
bright bachelor's button blue and bobbing
on the cold and hot winds of our breath,
as we make and unmake in passionate
diastole and systole the rhythm
of our unbound bonding, to have
and not to hold, to love
with minimized malice, hunger
and anger moment by moment balanced.

For Calling the Spirit Back from Wandering the Earth in its Human Feet

Joy Harjo

Put down that bag of potato chips, that white bread, that bottle of pop.

Turn off that cellphone, computer, and remote control.

Open the door, then close it behind you.

Take a breath offered by friendly winds. They travel the earth
gathering essences of plants to clean.

Give it back with gratitude.

If you sing it will give your spirit lift to fly to the stars' ears and
back.

Acknowledge this earth who has cared for you since you were
a dream planting itself precisely within your parents' desire.

Let your moccasin feet take you to the encampment of the
guardians who have known you before time, who will be
there after time. They sit before the fire that has been there
without time.

Let the earth stabilize your postcolonial insecure jitters.

Be respectful of the small insects, birds and animal people
who accompany you.
Ask their forgiveness for the harm we humans have brought
down upon them.

Don't worry.
The heart knows the way though there may be high-rises,
interstates, checkpoints, armed soldiers, massacres, wars, and
those who will despise you because they despise themselves.

The journey might take you a few hours, a day, a year, a few years, a hundred, a thousand, or even more.

Watch your mind. Without training it might run away and leave your heart for the immense human feast set by the thieves of time.

Do not hold regrets.

When you find your way to the circle, to the fire kept burning by the keepers of your soul, you will be welcomed.

You must clean yourself with cedar, sage, or other healing plant.

Cut the ties you have to failure and shame.

Let go the pain you are holding in your mind, your shoulders, your heart, all the way to your feet. Let go the pain of your ancestors to make way for those who are heading in our direction.

Ask for forgiveness.

Call upon the help of those who love you. These helpers take many forms: animal, element, bird, angel, saint, stone, or ancestor.

Call your spirit back. It may be caught in corners and creases of shame, judgement, and human abuse.

You must call in a way that your spirit will want to return. Speak to it as you would to a beloved child.

Welcome your spirit back from its wandering. It may return in pieces, in tatters. Gather them together. They will be happy to be found after being lost for so long.

Your spirit will need to sleep awhile after it is bathed and given clean clothes.

Now you can have a party. Invite everyone you know who loves and supports you. Keep room for those who have no place else to go.

Make a giveaway, and remember, keep the speeches short.

Then, you must do this: help the next person find their way through the dark.

Mimesis

Fady Joudah

My daughter
                    wouldn't hurt a spider
That had nested
Between her bicycle handles
For two weeks
She waited
Until it left of its own accord

If you tear down the web I said
It will simply know
This isn't a place to call home
And you'd get to go biking

She said that's how others
Become refugees isn't it?

There Was a Time I Would Reject Those

Muhyiddin Ibn Al-'Arabi

There was a time I would reject those
who were not of my faith.
But now, my heart has grown capable
of taking on all forms.
It is a pasture for gazelles,
An abbey for monks.
A table for the Torah,
Kaaba for the pilgrim.
My religion is love.
Whichever the route love's caravan shall take,
That shall be the path of my faith.

Journey

Linda Hogan

The mouth of the river may be beautiful.
It doesn't remember the womb of its beginning.
It doesn't look back to where it's been
or wonder who ahead of it polished the rough stones.

It is following the way
in its fullness,
now like satin,
now cresting,
waters meeting, kindred
to travel gathered together,
all knowing it flows
one way, shining or in shadows.
And me, the animal
I ride wants to drive forward,
its longing not always my own,
overrunning its banks and bounds,
edgeless, spilling along the way

because, as I forget,
it knows everything
is before it.

On Pilgrimage

Czeslaw Milosz

May the smell of thyme and lavender accompany us on our journey
To a province that does not know how lucky it is
For it was, among all the hidden corners of the earth,
The only one chosen and visited.

We tended toward the Place but no signs led there.
Till it revealed itself in a pastoral valley
Between mountains that look older than memory,
By a narrow river humming at the grotto.

May the taste of wine and roast meat stay with us
As it did when we used to feast in the clearings,
Searching, not finding, gathering rumors,
Always comforted by the brightness of the day.

May the gentle mountains and the bells of the flocks
Remind us of everything we have lost,
For we have seen on our way and fallen in love
With the world that will pass in a twinkling.

Lourdes, 1976

In Early Evening

Kirsten Dierking

Everything
around the lake

assents to silence.
All birds

agree to hush.
All feathers, all fur,

are felted thick
with fading light.

The boat comes
to a gentle rest

on the blue cusp
of still water.

Take it with you,
this interlude,

the sweet middle eye
of the storm.

Seas

Juan Ramón Jiménez

I have a feeling that my boat
has struck, down there in the depths,
against a great thing.
And nothing
happens! Nothing . . . Silence . . . Waves. . . .

—Nothing happens? Or has everything happened,
and are we standing now, quietly, in the new life?

blessing the boats

Lucille Clifton

(at St. Mary's)

may the tide
that is entering even now
the lip of our understanding
carry you out
beyond the face of fear
may you kiss
the wind then turn from it
certain that it will
love your back   may you
open your eyes to water
water waving forever
and may you in your innocence
sail through this to that

Smart Cookie

Richard Schiffman

after Wallace Stevens

The fortune that you seek is in another cookie,
was my fortune. So I'll be equally frank—the wisdom
that you covet is in another poem. The life that you desire
is in a different universe. The cookie you are craving
is in another jar. The jar is buried somewhere in Tennessee.
Don't even think of searching for it. If you found that jar,
everything would go kerflooey for a thousand miles around.
It is the jar of your fate in an alternate reality. Don't even
think of living that life. Don't even think of eating that cookie.
Be a smart cookie—eat what's on your plate, not in some jar
in Tennessee. That's my wisdom for today, though I know
it's not what you were looking for.

Notes on the Poems

Reading mindfulness poets from diverse backgrounds can expand our understanding of what it means to be present in the here and now. However, when we are unfamiliar with a poet's culture, language, or mode of expression, we sometimes need a little help to engage more fully with his or her text. A special thanks to the following authors for briefly providing some context to illuminate their poems.

"Lakol Wicoun" by Lydia Whirlwind Soldier (p. 69): *Lakol wicoun* is the Lakota way of life. It means living one's life in the best possible way, every day. Traditionally, Lakota elders teach every *takoja*, grandchild, how to live in this manner, respecting the laws of *Unci Maka*, Grandmother Earth.

"Versions of Ghalib: Ghazal I" by Ghalib (p. 82): Ghalib (1797-1869) was born in India and wrote in Urdu. He specialized in the ghazal, a form of poetry that originated in seventh-century Arabia. Poet and translator Ruth L. Schwartz based this trio of poems on a prose translation of Ghalib's "Ghazal #1," published by Aijaz Ahmad and published in the book *Ghazals by Ghalib* (Columbia University Press, 1971).

"*Minobimaadizi*" by Kimberly Blaeser (p. 118): "Anishinaabeg people," Blaeser writes, "have always sought *minobimaadizi*, a way of living well in the world. Now the *bawaajigan* or dream involves mending the broken elements of our relationship and restoring balance among the four elements: *aki* (earth), *nabi* (the waters), *ishkode* (fire), and *noodin* (wind). Therefore, we offer *nanaandawi'iwe-nagamon*, healing songs, for ourselves and our world. Ceremony and language both become *mashkiki*, medicine; and we invoke the strength of clans as we work for wellness: *mino-ayaa*, s/he is well. We reclaim that sacred balance."

"Wakarusa Medicine Wheel" by Denise Low (p. 132): Art students of Haskell Indian Nations University joined with Leslie Evans and earthworks artist Stan Herd in 1992 to create the Wakarusa Medicine Wheel in the wetlands of the Wakarusa River, in Kansas. The circle, marking the astrological locations of the summer and winter solstices, represents the death, rebirth, balance and healing in Mother Earth. The spokes are the four directions, marked by stone pillars that help visitors to remember the four seasons and their spiritual qualities. Offerings made to the directions show the continuing life of native traditions. A thunderbird, located to the east, points to the sacred circle and sacred fire.

About the Poets

Dick Allen, author of nine poetry collections, has had poems in *Poetry*, *The New Yorker*, *Atlantic Monthly*, *Hudson Review*, *Tricycle*, and in many national anthologies. He's received a Pushcart Prize, N.E.A. and Ingram Merrill Poetry writing fellowships, and The New Criterion Poetry Book Award for *This Shadowy Place* (St. Augustine's Press, 2014). He was the Connecticut State Poet Laureate from 2010-2015. His newest collection is *Zen Master Poems* (Wisdom, Inc., 2016).

Yehuda Amichai (1924–2000) was born Ludwig Pfeuffer in Germany. He became one of Israel's finest poets and the most translated Hebrew-language poet since King David. His poems explore such difficult themes as war, nationhood, Jewish identity, God, religion, love and sex.

Archie Randolph (A. R.) Ammons (1926-2001), a major American poet and long-time professor at Cornell University, was born in the cotton and tobacco-growing region of North Carolina. Deeply influenced by Transcendentalism, he was preoccupied as a poet with humanity's relationship to nature. Among other major honors, he won the annual National Book Award for Poetry in 1973 and 1993.

Craig Arnold (1967-2009) was a musician and award-winning poet who taught at the University of Wyoming. He authored two collections of poetry, *Shells* (1999) and *Made Flesh* (2008). He disappeared in 2009 while hiking alone on a Japanese island, where he was researching a book of poems he hoped to write. His body was never recovered.

Margaret Atwood is the celebrated author of more than forty books of fiction, poetry, and critical essays. Canadian-born, she lives in Toronto with writer Graeme Gibson. She has received nearly sixty awards in her home country and internationally. Her most recent volume of poetry is *The Door* (2007). (*www.margaretatwood.ca*)

Jimmy Santiago Baca is an award-winning poet and writer of Apache and Chicano descent, originally from New Mexico. A self-styled "poet of the people," he first wrote poetry as a young man in prison. Through his nonprofit organization Cedar Tree, Inc., he conducts writing workshops across the country on reservations and in school settings, barrio community centers, housing projects and correctional facilities. (*www.jimmysantiagobaca.com*)

Rebecca Baggett's most recent collections are *God Puts on the Body of a Deer* (Main Street Rag) and *Thalassa* (Finishing Line Press). New poems appear or are forthcoming in *Cold Mountain Review*, *The Dead Mule School of Southern Literature*, *Miramar*, *and New Ohio Review*. She lives in Athens, Georgia.

Tom Barrett is a licensed professional counselor living in Portland, Oregon. He is an occasional poet and the longtime keeper of the website *Interlude: An Internet Retreat* (*www.interluderetreat.com*). He has been a proponent of meditation for many years and incorporates mindfulness into his work with clients at a hospital-based outpatient mental health clinic.

Anita Barrows has five published volumes of poetry, including *We Are the Hunger* (Kelsey Books, 2017). Her translations from French, Italian and German have been published by British and American presses, and she has won numerous awards for both her poems and her translations. She lives in Berkeley, California, where she is a clinical psychologist and a Professor at The Wright Institute. A mother and grandmother, she shares her household with dogs, cats and birds.

Ellen Bass had her most recent book of poetry, *Like a Beggar*, published in 2014 by Copper Canyon Press. In addition to poetry, she has written highly successful nonfiction books that address LBGT youth and women survivors of child sexual abuse. The recipient of many awards, she has taught poetry and creative writing at many locations, nationally and internally. She currently teaches in the low residency MFA program at Pacific University. (*www.ellenbass.com*)

Wendell Berry is a poet, novelist, essayist and environmentalist with one primary message: Either we humans will learn to respect and live in harmony with the natural rhythms of this planet, or we will perish. He lives and farms near his Kentucky birthplace. His volumes of poetry affirm and celebrate the holiness of everyday life. (*www.wendellberrybooks.com*)

Kimberly Blaeser, writer, photographer, and scholar, is author of three poetry collections—most recently *Apprenticed to Justice*; and editor of *Traces in Blood, Bone, and Stone: Contemporary Ojibwe Poetry*. A UW-Milwaukee professor of Creative Writing and Native American Literature, she serves on faculty for the Institute of American Indian Arts low rez MFA and was Wisconsin Poet Laureate for 2015-16. An enrolled member of the Minnesota Chippewa Tribe, she grew up on White Earth Reservation.

Chana Bloch (1940-2017) passed away while *Poetry of Presence* was in production. A longtime Professor of English at Mills College, she was the author of award-winning books of poetry, translation, and scholarship. From 2007-2012 she served as the first Poetry Editor of *Persimmon Tree*, an online journal of the arts by women over sixty. Her sixth and final poetry collection, *The Moon Is Almost Full*, is due out in September.

Robert Bly is an award-winning American poet, editor, translator, essayist, storyteller and activist. Born into a Norwegian community in western Minnesota, he served as that state's first poet laureate. As a writer, he is perhaps best known for his book *Iron John: A Book about Men*, a foundational work in the mythopoetic men's movement in the U.S. (*www.robertbly.com*)

John Brantingham is the author of seven books of poetry and fiction including *The Green of Sunset*. He and his wife live off grid in Sequoia and Kings Canyon National Parks in the summer where they teach poetry and painting. He is currently working on a poetry collection about living in nature.

Judy Sorum Brown is a poet, speaker, writer, and educator whose work focuses on leadership and the nature of change. She has designed and facilitated leadership programs and retreats for symphony orchestras, urban libraries, manufacturing plants, public schools, the federal government, and those who serve elders. Along with several leadership books, she has authored three volumes of poetry: *The Sea Accepts All Rivers & other poems*, *Simple Gifts* and *Steppingstones*. (*www.judysorumbrown.com*)

Linda Buckmaster wrote "Flowering" almost fifteen years ago on the Aran Islands. "Although the details of landscape may vary from place to place wherever I travel," she says, "the basics of this life (especially stone and bees) remain the same, especially in my homeplace of Mid-coast Maine. At the time of writing, the freshest loss with was my husband's sudden death. With subsequent losses over the years, I find the poem serves as a necessary reminder on how to live."

David Budbill (1940-2016) was born in Cleveland, Ohio, to a streetcar driver and a minister's daughter. He lived in the mountains of northern Vermont, authoring plays, essays, short story and poetry collections, a children's picture book, even the libretto for an opera. His final book of poems was *Happy Feet* (2011). (*www.davidbudbill.com*)

Charles Bukowski (1920-1994) was born Heinrich Karl Bukowski in Germany to an American father and a German mother who met after World War I. His family came to the U.S. when he was three. He lived most of his life in Los Angeles, producing thousands of poems, hundreds of short stories and six novels. Among his primary subjects were the daily lives of working class Americans, the drudgery of toil, alcoholism and relationships with women.

Grace Butcher taught English for 25 years at Kent State University at Geauga. A former US track champion at 800m, she is still running at age eighty-three. The "love of her life" is her horse Spencer, whom she rides and trains daily. She also acts at her community theater. Her poetry has appeared in many magazines and anthologies. Her latest collection is *Deer in the Mall*.

Julie Cadwallader Staub was born in Minneapolis, Minnesota. Her favorite words to hear growing up were, "Now you girls go outside and play." She found her way home to Vermont twenty-five years ago. Her poems have won awards, been featured on *The Writer's Almanac*, published in journals, and included in anthologies. Her poem "Milk" won Hunger Mountain's 2015 Ruth Stone Poetry Prize. Her first collection, *Face to Face*, was published by Cascadia in 2010. Her upcoming collection, *Wing Over Wing*, will be published by Paraclete Press in 2019.

Neil Carpathios has authored four full-length poetry collections, most recently, *Confessions of a Captured Angel* (Terrapin Books, 2016). His chapbooks were published as the result of national competition awards, most recently, *The Function of Sadness* (Slipstream Press, 2015). He edited the anthology *Every River on Earth: Writing from Appalachian Ohio* (Ohio University Press, 2015). In 2015 he was awarded his fourth Ohio Arts Council Individual Excellence Award in Poetry. He teaches at Shawnee State University in Portsmouth, Ohio.

Raymond Carver (1938-1988), a native of the American northwest, was a short-story writer and poet. His style was spare and intense. "Late Fragment" is the final poem in his last published work, *A New Path to the Waterfall*, written while he was dying of lung cancer. It is engraved on his tombstone.

Lucille Clifton (1936-2010), a prize-winning poet and author, was born Thelma Lucille Sayles in New York State. Among her poetry collections are *Blessing the Boats: New and Selected Poems 1988–2000*, which won the National Book Award. Twice nominated for the Pulitzer Prize for Poetry, she taught widely and also served as poet laureate for the state of Maryland (1979-1985).

Phyllis Cole-Dai is a writer, editor, songwriter, composer, public speaker—basically any profession that doesn't pay well. *Poetry of Presence* is the seventh book she has authored or edited. She and her husband reside in their adopted state of South Dakota with their teenage son, the joy of their lives. (*www.phylliscoledai.com*)

Billy Collins served as U.S. Poet Laureate from 2001 to 2003, and as the New York State Poet Laureate from 2004 to 2006. One of the most decorated and popular poets in America, he has authored sixteen books of poetry, his latest being *The Rain in Portugal* (2016). He is a Distinguished Professor of English at Lehman College of the City University of New York. (*www.billycollinspoetry.com*)

Barbara Crooker's work has appeared in a variety of literary journals, including *Common Wealth: Contemporary Poets on Pennsylvania* and *The Bedford Introduction to Literature*. She is the author of eight books of poetry; *Les Fauves* is the most recent. She has received a number of awards, including the 2004 W. B. Yeats Society of New York Award, the 2003 Thomas Merton Poetry of the Sacred Award, and three Pennsylvania Council on the Arts Creative Writing Fellowships.

Mahmoud Darwish (1941-2008), one of the most acclaimed poets in today's Arab world, was considered Palestine's national poet. He published more than thirty volumes of poetry and prose, which have been translated into dozens of languages, including Hebrew. Author of the Palestinian Declaration of Independence, he was also an award-winning human rights advocate.

Kirsten Dierking is the author of three books of poetry: *Tether*, *Northern Oracle* and *One Red Eye*. Her poems have frequently been read on the radio program *The Writer's Almanac*, and in 2015 she appeared as a guest on NPR's *A Prairie Home Companion*.

Born in Sioux City, Iowa, **David Allan Evans** taught at South Dakota State University for thirty-nine years. He also taught in China twice as a Fulbright Scholar. Nine collections of his poems have been published. He and his wife Jan moved back to the Sioux City area a couple of years ago.

Patricia Fargnoli, a former New Hampshire Poet Laureate, has published five full collections and three chapbooks. Her latest book is *Hallowed: New & Selected Poems* (Tupelo Press, 2017). She has won the Shelia Motton Award, the New Hampshire Literary Award for Poetry, and the ForeWord Magazine Silver Award for poetry. A MacDowell Fellow, she has published widely in such journals as *Alaska Quarterly*, *Rattle*, *Massachusetts Review*, and *Ploughshares*.

Julia Fehrenbacher is an author, a poet and a painter who is always looking for ways to spread a little good around in this world. She is the author of two books of poetry, *On the Other Side of Fear* and an e-book entitled *She Will Not Be Quiet*. She lives in Corvallis, Oregon, with her husband and two girls.

Laura Foley is the author of six poetry collections, including *WTF*, *Joy Street*, *Syringa and Night Ringing*. Her poem "Gratitude List" won the Common Good Books Poetry Contest judged by Garrison Keillor. "Nine Ways of Looking at Light" won the Joe Gouveia Outermost Poetry Contest, judged by Marge Piercy. A palliative care volunteer, she lives with her partner, Clara Gimenez, and three big dogs among the hills of Vermont. (*www.laurafoley.net*)

Ghalib (1797-1869), born Mirza Asadullah Beg Khan, was a well-known 18th-century poet who wrote in Urdu and Persian. He specialized in the ghazal, a form of poetry which originated in 7th-century Arabia.

Khalil Gibran (1883-1931) was a Lebanese-born essayist, novelist, poet and artist. He is perhaps best known for *The Prophet*, a book of poetic essays, including "On Pain." His works, written in both Arabic and English, are very lyrical and expressive of his religious and mystical sensibility.

Nikki Giovanni is the award-winning author of numerous children's books and poetry collections. Since 1987 she has taught at Virginia Tech, where she is University Distinguished Professor. "I don't have a lot of friends but I have good ones. I have a son and a granddaughter.... I like to cook, travel and dream. I'm a writer. I'm happy." (*www.nikki-giovanni.com*)

Rafael Jesús González taught Creative Writing & Literature at Laney College, Oakland, where he founded the Mexican & Latin American Studies Department. Thrice nominated for a Pushcart Prize, he was honored by the National Council of Teachers of English for his writing in 2003. His book of poems *La Musa Lunática/The Lunatic Muse* (Pandemonium Press, Berkeley, California) was published in 2009, and in 2015 the City of Berkeley honored him with a Lifetime Achievement Award. (*www.rjgonzalez.blogspot.com*)

Charles Goodrich is the author of three books of poetry, *A Scripture of Crows*; *Going to Seed: Dispatches from the Garden*; and *Insects of South Corvallis*. He also co-edited two anthologies, *Forest Under Story: Creative Inquiry in an Old-Growth Forest* and *In the Blast Zone: Catastrophe and Renewal on Mount St. Helens*. Following a long career as a professional gardener, he now directs the Spring Creek Project for Ideas, Nature, and the Written Word.

Louise Glück, born in New York City of Hungarian-Jewish heritage, served as the twelfth U.S. Poet Laureate. She won the 1993 Pulitzer Prize for Poetry for *The Wild Iris*. Her most recent collection, *Faithful and Virtuous Night*, won the 2014 National Book Award in Poetry. She currently teaches as a writer-in-residence at Yale University and in the creative writing program at Boston University.

Mary Gray, a native of Portland, Oregon, has worked as an English teacher and as a journalist. Her poems have appeared in many literary journals and magazines. A book of her poems is scheduled for publication in early September, 2017. She currently teaches poetry writing at the Portland Art Museum.

Hafiz (1310?-1390), or Hafez, is a celebrated Persian poet. Born Khwāja Shams-ud-Dīn Muhammad Hāfez-e Shīrāzī, "Hafiz" is a title, meaning "one who has learned the Qur'an by heart." A Sufi Muslim, he is lauded for writing a complex form of lyric poetry called the ghazal. Traditionally set to music, ghazals are characterized by melancholy, love, longing, and metaphysical questions. Hafiz's poetry has been popularized by Daniel Ladinsky, one of the foremost English-language interpreters of his work.

Thich Nhat Hanh is a Vietnamese Buddhist monk, spiritual leader and peace activist who is revered globally for his powerful teachings and bestselling writings on mindfulness and peacemaking. Dr. Martin Luther King, Jr., nominated him for the Nobel Peace Prize in 1967. Now living at Plum Village, his mindfulness practice center in southern France, he has published over a hundred books. (*www.plumvillage.org/about/thich-nhat-hanh*)

Twyla M. Hansen is Nebraska's State Poet. She co-directs the *Poetry from the Plains: A Nebraska Perspective* website. Her newest poetry book is *Rock • Tree • Bird* (Backwaters Press, 2017). Two of her books have won Nebraska Book Awards, including *Potato Soup*, a Nebraska 150 Notable Book for the 2017 Sesquicentennial. Her writing has appeared widely in periodicals, newspapers, anthologies, and many other publications.

Joy Harjo, a member of the Mvskoke Nation, is a celebrated poet, storyteller, musician, memoirist, playwright and activist. Her seven books of poetry have garnered many awards, including the Lifetime Achievement Award from the Native Writers Circle of the Americas, and the William Carlos Williams Award from the Poetry Society of America. She lives in Albuquerque, New Mexico. (*www.joyharjo.com*)

Penny Harter's recent books include *The Resonance Around Us* (2013); *One Bowl* (2012); and *Recycling Starlight* (2010; reprint 2017). Recent work has appeared, or is forthcoming, in a number of journals and anthologies. She has won three fellowships from the New Jersey State Council on the Arts, and the Mary Carolyn Davies Award from the Poetry Society of America. She lives in the southern New Jersey shore area.

With fifteen books in print, **Linda M. Hasselstrom** writes and conducts writing retreats in person and by email from her South Dakota ranch. Her newest book is *The Wheel of the Year: A Writer's Workbook*, containing two years' worth of writing suggestions and examples. (*www.windbreakhouse.com, www.windbreakhouse.wordpress.com*)

Seamus Heaney (1939-2013), born in County Derry, Northern Ireland, was widely regarded as a preeminent twentieth-century poet. He was also a playwright, translator, and lecturer. Among many other awards, he received the 1995 Nobel Prize in Literature "for works of lyrical beauty and ethical depth, which exalt everyday miracles and the living past." He taught at both Oxford and Harvard.

Tom Hennen was born into a big Dutch-Irish family in Minnesota and grew up on a farm. He began his adult work life as a letterpress and offset printer, but switched careers. He is now retired from his post as wildlife technician at the Sand Lake National Wildlife Refuge in South Dakota. A heralded "poet of the landscape" and master of the prose poem, Hennen's latest poetry collection is *Darkness Sticks to Everything* (2013).

Donna Hilbert's latest book is *The Congress of Luminous Bodies*, from Aortic Books. Her work is anthologized in *Boomer Girls, A New Geography of Poets, Solace in So Many Words, The Widows' Handbook* (Kent State University Press), and *The Doll Collection* (Terrapin Books), among others. Her poems can be found monthly in the online magazine Verse-Virtual.com. She writes and leads workshops in Long Beach, California. (*www.donnahilbert.com*)

Judyth Hill, poet, teacher, author and editor, lives in Colorado, teaches at writing conferences world 'round, offers classes and online editing at www.judythhill.com, and global WildWriting Culinary Adventures at www.eat-write-travel.com. She has authored nine books of poetry. Her internationally acclaimed poem, "Wage Peace," has been published worldwide, set to music, and performed and recorded by national choirs and orchestras. The *St. Helena Examiner* described her as "Energy with skin"; the *Denver Post* as "A tigress with a pen."

Chicago-born **Edward Hirsch** has published eight books of poems and five prose books on poetry, including *How to Read a Poem and Fall in Love with Poetry*, a national bestseller. *The Living Fire: New and Selected Poems* (2010) brings together thirty-five years of his work. A recipient of numerous awards and fellowships, he is now president of the John Simon Guggenheim Memorial Foundation. (*www.edwardhirsch.com*)

Jane Hirshfield, who lives in the San Francisco Bay Area, is an acclaimed poet, essayist, editor, translator, and educator. She has authored eight collections of poetry and received numerous awards. Deeply influenced by Zen Buddhism, her work consistently addresses themes of social and environmental justice, and exhibits profound empathy for the suffering of living beings. (*www.janehirshfield.com*)

Tony Hoagland, who hails from North Carolina and a series of military bases in the American South, is an essayist and prize-winning author of five volumes of witty, poignant poetry commenting on contemporary American life and culture. A teacher at the University of Houston, he regards poems as not just the most economical of literary forms but also the most emotionally intimate, which is why many of us turn to it during times of hardship.

Linda Hogan, a member of the Chickasaw Nation, is an internationally recognized public speaker and writer of poetry, fiction, and essays. Her main interests as both writer and scholar are environmental issues, indigenous spiritual traditions and cultures, and Southeastern tribal histories. In 2007 she was inducted into the Chickasaw Nation Hall of Fame. (*www.lindahoganwriter.com*)

Miroslav Holub (1923-1998) was an internationally known Czech poet noted for his detached, lyrical reflections on humanist and scientific subjects. Though a prolific creative writer, he considered science his true profession, researching and writing as a clinical pathologist and immunologist. His medical background is evident in much of his poetry, which has been widely translated.

Sheri Hostetler is a Mennonite pastor, poet, and mother. She first learned mindfulness (although it wasn't called that) growing up in a small, rural Amish-Mennonite community in Ohio. She now attempts to pastor and parent mindfully in the San Francisco Bay Area.

Marie Howe, an award-winning poet from New York, says that the most difficult task for us today might be "not to look away from what is actually happening. To put down the iPod and the e-mail and the phone. To look long enough so that we can look through it—like a window." She currently teaches at Sarah Lawrence College, New York University, and Columbia University. (*www.mariehowe.com*)

Albert Huffstickler (1927-2002) lived much of his life in Austin, Texas, where he was known as the "Bard of Hyde Park" and had a tremendous network of friends. A great believer in small presses, he published hundreds of poems in chapbooks printed locally and in journals around the world, from the academic to the underground. He also had his own imprint, Press of Circumstance. In his later years, he worked actively as a visual artist.

Holly J. Hughes is author of *Passings* (Expedition Press, 2016), *Sailing by Ravens* (University of Alaska Press, 2014), co-author of *The Pen and The Bell: Mindful Writing in a Busy World* (Skinner House Press, 2012), and editor of the anthology, *Beyond Forgetting: Poetry and Prose about Alzheimer's Disease* (Kent State University Press, 2009). She teaches writing and mindfulness workshops where she lives on the Olympic peninsula in Washington state. (*www.hollyjhughes.com*)

Muhyiddin Ibn Al-'Arabi (1165-1240) was a Muslim mystic, philosopher, sage and poet born of Arab parents in Spain. Revered as a great spiritual master, he travelled extensively on pilgrimage throughout the Islamic world. He wrote over 350 works, including some of the finest poetry in the Arabic language. Rooted in the Qur'an, he argued for the Unity of Being and the belief that each person has a unique path to the truth, which unites all paths in itself.

Juan Ramón Jiménez (1881-1958) was a prolific Spanish poet, editor, and critic. When the Spanish Civil War broke out in 1936, he and his wife went into exile. They spent most of their remaining years in Puerto Rico. His lyrical poetry won him the Nobel Prize for Literature in 1956.

Erica Jong is an American novelist, poet, essayist and teacher known for her fierce commitment to women's rights. She consistently uses her crafts to help women forge a feminist consciousness. Among other awards she has been honored with the United Nations Award for Excellence in Literature. A poet at heart, she believes that words can save the world. (*www.ericajong.com*)

Fady Joudah was born in Texas to Palestinian refugees. He grew up in Libya and Saudi Arabia before returning to the U.S. to study medicine. He has authored several volumes of poetry and is also an award-winning poetry translator. In addition to writing poetry, he serves as an emergency room physician in Houston, Texas, and volunteers for Doctors Without Borders.

Kabir (1440?-1518?) was an iconoclastic Indian mystic and poet revered today as a saint by many Hindus, Muslims and Sikhs. He composed his wisdom poems or songs orally. They were transmitted in the same way until finally written down in the seventeenth century. Relentlessly critical of blind adherence to religion, he called upon his contemporaries to be utterly faithful to the Divine, which manifests in all creatures.

Stuart Kestenbaum, Poet Laureate of Maine, is the author of four volumes of poetry and a collection of essays. He is the former longtime director of the Haystack Mountain School of Crafts in Deer Isle, Maine, where he established innovative programs combining craft, writing, and new technologies. The brother he mentions in "Prayer for the Dead" was lost in the destruction of the World Trade Center on September 11, 2001.

Galway Kinnell (1927-2014), born in Rhode Island, was a Pulitzer Prize-winning poet as well as a translator, novelist, children's book author, teacher and social activist. The author of ten books of poetry, he taught for many years at New York University, where he was Erich Maria Remarque Professor of Creative Writing. He had the honor of serving as the poet laureate for Vermont (1989-1993). (*www.galwaykinnell.com*)

Iowa-born **Ted Kooser**, a former life insurance executive, is a Pulitzer Prize-winning poet who served two terms as U.S. Poet Laureate. He currently edits "American Life in Poetry," a weekly newspaper column with an estimated circulation of three and a half million readers around the world (www.americanlifeinpoetry.org). He also teaches half-time at The University of Nebraska. (*www.tedkooser.net*)

Danusha Laméris's work has been featured, or is forthcoming in, *The Best American Poetry*, *The New York Times*, *The American Poetry Review*, *New Letters*, and *The Sun*, as well by Garrison Keillor on *The Writer's Almanac*. Her first book, *The Moons of August* (2014), was chosen by Naomi Shihab Nye as the winner of the Autumn House Press poetry prize. She lives in Santa Cruz, California and teaches private writing workshops. (*www.danushalameris.com*)

Dorianne Laux of Maine is the prize-winning author of five poetry collections and co-author of the celebrated text *The Poet's Companion: A Guide to the Pleasures of Writing Poetry* (W. W. Norton, 1997). She teaches poetry at North Carolina State University and is a founding faculty member of Pacific University's low residency MFA program. (*www.doriannelaux.com*)

Li-Young Lee was born of Chinese parents in Jakarta, Indonesia, and settled with his family in the U.S. while a young boy. He is the author of four critically-acclaimed books of poetry, the most recent being *Behind My Eyes*. His honors include fellowships from the National Endowment for the Arts, The Lannan Foundation, and the John Simon Guggenheim Memorial Foundation. He now lives in Chicago with his wife and their two sons.

Denise Levertov (1923-1997) was an English-born poet, essayist and social activist who lived most of her adult life in the U.S. She published more than twenty volumes of poetry. Her later work was influenced by her conversion to Roman Catholicism. She taught for many years at Stanford University and spent the last decade of her life writing in Seattle, Washington.

Annie Lighthart is a poet and teacher who started writing poetry after her first visit to an Oregon old-growth forest. She has taught at Boston College and in writing workshops with students of all ages. Poems from her book *Iron String* have been read on *The Writer's Almanac*, turned into choral music, used in projects in Ireland and New Zealand, and have traveled farther than she has.

Carolyn Locke lives in Maine and is a graduate of the MFA in Creative Writing Program at Goddard College. She is the author of *Always This Falling* (2010), *Not One Thing: Following Matsuo Basho's Journey to the Interior* (2013), and *The Place We Become* (2015).

Denise Low is former Kansas Poet Laureate and past board president of the Associated Writers and Writing Programs. The University of Nebraska Press is publishing her 2017 memoir, *The Turtle's Beating Heart*, about her grandfather's Lenape heritage. Other recent books are *Mélange Block: Poems*, *Jackalope* (short fiction), and *Natural Theologies: Essays*. Among numerous honors she has won three Kansas Notable Book Awards and the Pami Jurassi Bush Award of the Academy of American Poets. She co-publishes Mammoth Publications. (*www.deniselow.net*)

Alison Luterman's three books of poetry are *The Largest Possible Life*, *See How We Almost Fly*, and *Desire Zoo*. She has also written an e-book of personal essays, *Feral City*; half a dozen plays; and a new musical, *The Chain*. She performs with the Oakland-based improvisation troupe *Wing It!*, teaches memoir and poetry at The Writing Salon in Berkeley, California, and has given writing workshops all over the U.S., including at Omega and Esalen Institutes. (*www.alisonluterman.net*)

Teddy Macker's first book of poetry—*This World* (foreword by Brother David Steindl-Rast)—appeared in March of 2015 through White Cloud Press. A lecturer at University of California-Santa Barbara and orchardist, he lives with his wife and daughters on a small farm in the foothills of Carpinteria, California.

Freya Manfred's sixth collection of poetry, *Swimming With A Hundred Year Old Snapping Turtle*, won the 2009 Midwest Bookseller's Choice Award. Her eighth collection is *Speak, Mother* (2015). Her award-winning poetry has appeared in over 100 reviews and magazines and over fifty anthologies. Her memoir, *Frederick Manfred: A Daughter Remembers*, was nominated for a Minnesota Book Award and an Iowa Historical Society Award. Her new memoir is *Raising Twins: A True Life Adventure* from Nodin Press. (*www.freyamanfredwriter.com*)

William Stanley (W. S.) Merwin, a native of New York City, is a former U.S. Poet Laureate and two-time Pulitzer Prize winner. He has published more than fifty books of poetry, translation, and prose. For the past several decades he has lived and worked in Maui, Hawaii, where he has carefully restored the tropical forest surrounding his home, an old banana plantation. His Buddhist practice and environmentalism have profoundly influenced his work. (*www.merwinconservancy.org*)

Czeslaw Milosz (1911-2004), a native of Lithuania, was a Polish poet, writer, translator and diplomat. He spent most of World War II in Nazi-occupied Warsaw working for underground presses and giving aid to Jews. After the war, he sought political asylum in France. In 1960 he moved to the U.S. to teach Slavic languages and literatures at the University of California at Berkeley. His work was banned in Poland until 1980, when he won the Nobel Prize for Literature.

Marilyn Nelson, born in Cleveland, Ohio, is the prize-winning author or translator of more than twenty-four books. Her latest poetry collection is *Faster Than Light* (2012). She is a professor emerita of English at the University of Connecticut and was poet laureate of Connecticut from 2001 to 2006. In 2012 the Poetry Society of America honored her with the Frost Medal, its most prestigious award, for "distinguished lifetime achievement in poetry." (*www.marilyn-nelson.com*)

Howard Nemerov (1920-1991), born to Russian Jewish parents in New York City, was a two-time U.S. Poet Laureate. He authored numerous novels and collections of poetry and essays, winning the Pulitzer Prize for Poetry in 1977. He was Distinguished Professor of English and Distinguished Poet in Residence at Washington University in St. Louis from 1969 until his death.

Pablo Neruda (1904-1973), whose birth name was Ricardo Eliécer Neftalí Reyes Basoalto, led a passionate life of poetry writing, diplomacy, leftist political activity, and romance. A Chilean, he is widely regarded in Latin America as "the people's poet" and in Western literature as one of the greats. Among the many awards he received were the International Peace Prize in 1950 and the Nobel Prize for Literature in 1971.

Sister Dang Ngheim was ordained as a Buddhist nun by Thich Nhat Hanh. Born in central Vietnam during the Tet Offensive and raised there by her grandmother, she came to the U.S. in 1985, graduated from medical school and began working as a doctor, integrating Western and Eastern medical traditions. She is the author of *Healing: A Woman's Journey from Doctor to Nun* and *Mindfulness as Medicine: A Story of Healing Body and Spirit.*

Kathleen Norris is an award-winning poet, writer, and author of several New York Times bestselling memoirs about the spiritual life. Her books of poetry include *The Middle of the World, Little Girls in Church*, and *The Astronomy of Love*. Much of her work explores the theme that the spiritual is rooted in the chaos of daily life. Widowed in 2003, she now divides her time between South Dakota and Hawaii.

Naomi Shihab Nye was born to a Palestinian father and an American mother. Drawing on her Palestinian-American heritage, the cultural diversity of her home in Texas, and her experiences traveling and teaching in Asia, Europe, Canada, Mexico, and the Middle East, she uses her writing to attest to our shared humanity. She is the award-winning author and/or editor of more than thirty books.

Mary O'Connor spent many decades in teaching for her religious community, the Sisters of Mercy, and for various universities. Now retired, she works with the homeless in San Diego, and continues to give poetry retreats and workshops.

John O'Donohue (1956-2008) was a priest, philosopher, and poet born in County Clare, Ireland. His numerous books of "long form, prayer-style" poetry, composed mostly in a remote cottage in Connemara, grew out of contemplative practice, rigorous academic study and love for land and sea. After retiring from the priesthood, he devoted himself full-time to writing and a public life of speaking and advocating around the world for social justice. (*www.johnodonohue.com*)

Mary Oliver, a native of Ohio, was recently acknowledged by the *New York Times* as "far and away, this country's best-selling poet." Winner of the Pulitzer Prize among many other awards, she has published more than twenty volumes of poetry and a half-dozen of prose. She now lives in Florida after having resided in Provincetown, Massachusetts, for over fifty years. www.maryoliver.beacon.org

Gregory Orr, widely considered to be a master of short, lyric free verse, is the award-winning author of eleven collections of poetry. His most recent volumes include *The River Inside the River*, *How Beautiful The Beloved*, and *Concerning the Book that is the Body of the Beloved*. He is Professor of English at the University of Virginia, where he founded the MFA program in writing.

Joe Paddock, author of two poetry collections, is also an environmentalist, essayist, and oral historian. He lives with his wife Nancy Paddock in his childhood home in Litchfield, Minnesota. He has served as Community Poet for Olivia, Minnesota; as Regional Poet for the Southwestern Minnesota Arts and Humanities Council; as Poet-in-Residence for Minnesota Public Radio; and as Humanist in Residence for the American Farm Project of the National Farmers Union.

Nancy Paddock is a poet, playwright and oral historian who lives and gardens with husband Joe Paddock in her native Minnesota. Her collection *Trust the Wild Heart* was a finalist for the 2006 Minnesota Book Award in poetry. She is also the author of *A Song at Twilight: Of Alzheimer's and Love*, a memoir about her parents' lives, their Alzheimer's disease, and their deaths four days apart. Most recently, she released another volume of poetry, *Cooking with Pavarotti* (Red Dragonfly Press, 2012).

Linda Pastan, a native of New York City, has resided for most of her life in Potomac, Maryland. Her quiet lyrics delve into everyday life and often the darkness and anxieties lying just beneath its surface. Much decorated, she has published twelve books of poetry and is also an essayist. Her most recent poetry collection is *Insomnia* (W. W. Norton, 2015).

Octavio Paz (1914-1998), born into a family of writers in Mexico City, was a poet, essayist, and diplomat. Acclaimed as one of the major Latin American authors of the twentieth century, he produced more than thirty books. He was awarded the Cervantes Award in 1981, the Neustadt Prize in 1982, and the Nobel Prize for Literature in 1990. *The Poems of Octavio Paz* (2012) is a career-spanning collection of his poems in English translation.

Paulann Petersen, Oregon Poet Laureate Emerita, has six full-length books of poetry, most recently *Understory*, from Lost Horse Press. The Latvian composer Eriks Esenvalds chose a poem from her book *The Voluptuary* as the lyric for a choral composition that is now part of the repertoire of the Choir at Trinity College Cambridge.

Marge Piercy, born into a working-class family in Detroit, Michigan, is a poet, novelist, essayist, and activist. Her work is grounded in feminism, Jewish spirituality, and concern for social injustice. In addition to many novels, she has published nineteen books of poetry, including *Made in Detroit*, *The Crooked Inheritance*, and *The Hunger Moon: New and Selected Poems, 1980-2010*. She lives with her husband in Cape Cod, Massachusetts. (*www.margepiercy.com*)

Li Po (701–762) was a Chinese poet of the Tang Dynasty. He is one of the most popular of all Chinese poets. A restless fellow, he spent much of his life wandering and writing poetry, particularly on the themes of wine, women, and nature.

Massachusetts-born **Anne Porter** (1911-2011), mother of five, began writing poetry more seriously after the death of her painter husband, Fairfield Porter. She published the first of her three poetry books, *An Altogether Different Language*, when she was 83. It was a finalist for the National Book Award.

Jack Ridl's *Practicing to Walk Like a Heron* received the Foreword Reviews Gold Medal for Poetry. His other award-winning collections are *Broken Symmetry* and *Losing Season*. The Poetry Society of Michigan named him Honorary Chancellor, only the second poet so-named. He is co-author with Peter Schakel of *Approaching Literature*. Winner of the Gary Gildner Poetry Prize, he was named by the Carnegie Foundation as Michigan's Professor of the Year. More than 85 of his students are now publishing.

Rainer Maria Rilke (1875-1926), born in Prague, traveled widely in Europe, with Paris serving as the geographic center of his life until World War I. Thereafter he lived in Germany and finally Switzerland. By the time he died of leukemia, his work was intensely admired by many leading European artists but was almost unknown to the general reading public. Today he is universally regarded as a master of verse.

Alberto Ríos's latest collection of poems is *A Small Story About the Sky*, preceded by *The Dangerous Shirt* and *The Theater of Night*, winner of the PEN/Beyond Margins Award. A finalist for the National Book Award and recipient of the Western Literature Association Distinguished Achievement Award, Ríos has taught at Arizona State University for over thirty years. He is Arizona's inaugural poet laureate and a chancellor of the Academy of American Poets.

J. Allyn Rosser's fourth collection of poems, *Mimi's Trapeze*, appeared in 2014 from the University of Pittsburgh Press. Her work has been awarded the Morse Prize, the New Criterion Poetry Prize, and *Poetry* magazine's Bock and Wood Prizes. She has received fellowships from the Lannan Foundation, Guggenheim Foundation, National Endowment for the Arts, and Ohio Arts Council. She teaches at Ohio University, where she also served for eight years as editor of *New Ohio Review*.

Muriel Rukeyser (1913-1980), a native of New York City, was an award-winning poet whose work was deeply informed by the violence and injustice she saw in the United States and abroad. During a literary career spanning five decades, she was outspoken on human rights issues, yet she could also address the personal dimension of life with great empathy and joy. Her poetry was compiled in *Out of Silence: Selected Poems* (1992) and *The Collected Poems of Muriel Rukeyser* (2005). (*www.murielrukeyser.emuenglish.org*)

Rumi (1207-1273) was born in the region known today as Afghanistan. A Persian-language poet, Muslim scholar and teacher, and Sufi mystic, he lived most of his life in present-day Turkey. Translator Coleman Barks, who has described him as "one of the great souls, and one of the great spiritual teachers," says that Rumi "wants us to be more alive, to wake up.... He wants us to see our beauty, in the mirror and in each other."

Marjorie Saiser is the author of five books of poetry and co-editor of two anthologies. Her work has been published in *American Life in Poetry, The Writer's Almanac, Nimrod, Rattle.com, PoetryMagazine.com, RHINO, Chattahoochee Review, Poetry East, Poet Lore*, and other journals. She has received the WILLA Award and nominations for the Pushcart Prize.

Robyn Sarah's tenth collection, *My Shoes Are Killing Me*, won the 2015 Governor General's Award for poetry in Canada. Her poems have been widely anthologized and broadcast many times on Garrison Keillor's *The Writer's Almanac*. In fall 2017, Biblioasis Press will publish *Wherever We Mean to Be: Selected Poems, 1975-2015*, a substantial retrospective of her work. Poetry editor for Cormorant Books since 2011, she lives in Montreal.

May Sarton (1912-1995), a native of Belgium, immigrated with her family to the U.S. during World War I and grew up in Massachusetts. Her career as a prize-winning writer spread over nearly six decades. A poet, novelist, memoirist, and children's book author, she wrote openly about identifying as a lesbian at a time when few other writers risked it. She spent her later years in Maine, living and working by the sea, sometimes despite tremendous physical hardships.

Nancy Ann Schaefer is a retired university professor who lives in rural Maine with her husband, two dogs and three cats. Her poems have appeared in numerous journals, anthologies, and websites as well as Chicagoland libraries and PACE buses. A Pushcart Prize nominee, her poetry has been featured on WVIK Public Radio. Her second chapbook, *Living at Hope's Edge* (Tiger's Eye Press), is forthcoming. In her spare time, she volunteers at an animal shelter.

Richard Schiffman is the author of two spiritual biographies, a journalist and a poet whose first full-length book of poems, *What the Dust Doesn't Know*, was published by Salmon Poetry in 2017. He regards his mystically inspired poetry, which often focuses on the natural world, to be an extension of his work as an environmental reporter since loving the earth and understanding the threats which face it are both preconditions for saving it.

Pat Schneider, poet, playwright, and librettist, is the author of ten books, including *How the Light Gets In: Writing as a Spiritual Practice* and *Writing Alone & With Others*, both from Oxford University Press, and five books of poems. Founder of Amherst Writers & Artists, she was for thirty years adjunct faculty at Pacific School of Religion in Berkeley, California. Forthcoming is a new book of poems, *The Weight of Love*. (*www.patschneider.com*)

Larry Smith is a poet, novelist, biographer, and editor of Bottom Dog Press. A retired professor of Bowling Green State University, he and wife Ann are co-founders of Converging Paths Meditation Center in Ohio.

Kansas-born **William Stafford** (1914-1993), published more than sixty-five volumes of poetry and prose, beginning with the award-winning *Traveling Through the Dark*, published when he was forty-eight. In 1970 he held the position now known as U.S. Poet Laureate. For more than thirty years he taught at Lewis and Clark College in Oregon. His personal ritual was to compose a poem a day. (*www.williamstaffordarchives.org*)

Hannah Stephenson is a poet, editor, and instructor living in Columbus, Ohio (where she also runs a literary series called Paging Columbus). She is the author of *Cadence* (forthcoming from the Wick Poetry Center) and *In the Kettle, the Shriek*; series Co-Editor of *New Poetry from the Midwest*; and her writing has appeared in *The Atlantic, The Huffington Post, 32 Poems, The Journal*, and *Poetry Daily*. (*www.thestorialist.com*)

Joyce Sutphen grew up on a farm in Stearns County, Minnesota. Her first collection of poems, *Straight Out of View*, won the Barnard New Women Poets Prize, and her recent collection, *Modern Love & Other Myths* (2015), was a finalist for a Minnesota Book Award. Her latest collection, *The Green House*, will be released by Salmon Press in May, 2017. She is the second Minnesota Poet Laureate, succeeding Robert Bly.

Wislawa Szymborska (1923-2012) lived most of her life in Krakow, Poland. Her poetic output was modest (only about 350 poems) but well received by readers and critics. She was, among other things, a deeply personal and often humorous poet who unveiled the large truths that exist in ordinary, everyday things. In 1996 she won the Nobel Prize in Literature. (*www.szymborska.org.pl/en.html*)

John Tagliabue (1923-2006) was an Italian-born American poet and playwright. He taught for more than thirty-five years at Bates College in Lewiston, Maine. He authored several books of poetry, including *New and Selected Poems, 1942-1997* (National Poetry Foundation, 1998).

Ronald Stuart (R. S.) Thomas (1913-2000) ranks among the leading Welsh poets of the twentieth century. An Anglican priest, he wrote in a spare, meditative style, often setting his poems against the bleak landscape of his homeland. He was awarded the Queen's Gold Medal for Poetry in 1964 and the prestigious Lannan Lifetime Achievement Award for Literature in 1996.

Rosemerry Wahtola Trommer served as Colorado's Western Slope Poet Laureate (2015-17). Her work has appeared in *O Magazine, Rattle.com, TEDx*, in back alleys, on *A Prairie Home Companion*, and on river rocks around town. She has taught poetry for Think 360, Craig Hospital, Ah Haa School for the Arts, Camp Coca Cola, meditation retreats, 12-step recovery programs, hospice, and many other organizations. One word-mantra: *Adjust*.

Rev. Dr. Lynn Ungar is a writer, a Unitarian Universalist minister, and a dog trainer, not necessarily in that order. Her book of poetry, *Bread and Other Miracles*, is available at her website. (*www.lynnungar.com*)

David Wagoner, an Ohio-born writer, is the award-winning author of ten novels and more than twenty poetry collections. He also enjoys an excellent reputation as a teacher of writing. A resident of Bothell, Washington, he is regarded as the leading poet of the American Northwest and one of the most accomplished poets in the nation at large.

Derek Walcott (1930-2017), of the island nation of Saint Lucia, authored numerous collections of poetry, as well as essays and plays. In 1992 he received the Nobel Prize in Literature, the second Caribbean writer to win it. Other honors include a MacArthur Foundation "genius" award, a Royal Society of Literature award, and, in 1988, the Queen's Medal for Poetry. He taught literature and writing at Boston University for more than two decades.

Alice Walker, who was born in Georgia, the eighth and last child of sharecroppers, is an internationally celebrated writer, poet, and activist whose books include seven novels, four collections of short stories, four children's books, and volumes of essays and poetry. She won the Pulitzer Prize in Fiction in 1983 and the National Book Award. She lives in Mendocino, California. (*www.alicewalkersgarden.com*)

Laura Grace Weldon is the author of a poetry collection titled *Tending* and a handbook of alternative education, *Free Range Learning*. She works as an editor and lives on a small farm. Her background includes teaching nonviolence workshops, writing poetry with nursing home residents, facilitating support groups for abuse survivors, and teaching writing classes. (*www.lauragraceweldon.com*)

Lydia Whirlwind Soldier is a Sicangu Lakota born in Bad Nation on the Rosebud Indian Reservation in South Dakota. An enrolled member of the Rosebud Sioux Tribe and a Lakota speaker, she is a poet, nonfiction writer, business owner and recognized craftswoman. Holding a Master's in Education Administration from Pennsylvania State University, she also worked in education for thirty years. Her collection of poems, *Memory Songs*, was published in 1999 by the Center for Western Studies.

David Whyte grew up in Yorkshire, England, with a strong, imaginative influence from his Irish mother. He now makes his home in the Pacific Northwest of the U.S. The author of eight books of poetry and four of prose, he holds a degree in Marine Zoology and has traveled extensively, including working as a naturalist guide in the Galapagos Islands and leading anthropological and natural history expeditions in the Andes, Amazon and Himalaya. (*www.davidwhyte.com*)

Ruby R. Wilson is a poet and freelance writer who has published three poetry chapbooks. Her poems have been published in such anthologies as *Crazy Woman Creek* and *Action, Influence, Voice: Contemporary South Dakota Women*. In addition to capturing images with poetry, she is also a photographer and loves roaming the countryside with her camera. She lives in rural Brookings County and is an archivist in the South Dakota State University Archives & Special Collections Department. (*www.rubyrwilson.wordpress.com*)

Christopher Wiseman was born in England. In 1969 he moved to Canada, where he taught for thirty years and founded the Creative Writing program at the University of Calgary. He has produced ten books of poetry, had his work published in over a hundred literary magazines and anthologies, and been honored with many awards, including the Order of Canada and the Queen's Diamond Jubilee Medal. Now retired, he resides in Calgary.

Marianne Murphy Zarzana teaches English and directs the Creative Writing Program at Southwest Minnesota State University. Her work has appeared in *Notre Dame Magazine*, *AYearofBeingHere.com*, *Stoneboat Literary Review*, *Blue Earth Review*, *Minnesota River Review*, *Dust & Fire*, *UmbrellaJournal.com*, and elsewhere. She is married to writer James A. Zarzana, and they have a grown daughter. (*www.mariannezarzana.com*)

Al Zolynas has published three books of poetry: *The New Physics*, *Under Ideal Conditions*, and *The Same Air*. He is also the co-editor of two poetry anthologies: *Men of Our Time* and *The Poetry of Men's Lives: An International Anthology* (University of Georgia Press). A retired academic, he practices and teaches Zen meditation in Escondido, California, where he lives with his wife and two cats.

Index of Authors and Titles

Permissions

The editors wish to thank the following publishers and individuals for permission to reprint. Every reasonable effort was made to identify the copyright holders, procure licenses, and gather previous publication credits. We sincerely apologize for any errors or omissions.

"Listening Deeply" by Dick Allen. Copyright © 2016 by Dick Allen. First published in *Zen Master Poems* (Wisdom Books, 2016). Reprinted by permission of the author.

"The Place Where We Are Right" by Yehuda Amichai, from *The Selected Poetry of Yehuda Amichai*, translated by Chana Bloch and Stephen Mitchell. © 1986, 1996, 2013 by Chana Bloch and Stephen Mitchell. Used by permission of University of California Press.

"Still." Copyright © 1965 by A. R. Ammons, from *The Selected Poems, Expanded Edition* by A. R. Ammons. Used by permission of W. W. Norton & Company, Inc.

"Meditation on a Grapefruit" from *Poetry* (October 2009). Copyright © 2009 by Craig Arnold. Reprinted with the permission of The Permissions Company, Inc., on behalf of the Estate of Craig Arnold.

"The Moment" from *Morning in the Burned House: New Poems* by Margaret Atwood. Copyright © 1995 by Margaret Atwood. Reprinted by permission of Houghton Mifflin Harcourt Publishing Company. All rights reserved.

"This Day" by Jimmy Santiago Baca, from *Spring Poems Along the Rio Grande*, copyright © 2007 by Jimmy Santiago Baca. Reprinted by permission of New Directions Publishing Corp.

"Testimony" by Rebecca Baggett. Copyright © 1996 by Rebecca Baggett. First published in *Still Life with Children* (Pudding House Publications, 1996). Reprinted by permission of the author.

"What's in the Temple?" by Tom Barrett. Copyright © 1999 by Tom Barrett. First published on *InterludeRetreat.com*. Reprinted by permission of the author.

"Lessons from Darkness" by Anita Barrows. Reprinted by permission of the author.

"The Thing Is" from *Mules of Love*. Copyright © 2002 by Ellen Bass. Reprinted with the permission of The Permissions Company, Inc., on behalf of BOA Editions Ltd., www.boaeditions.org.

"How to Be a Poet." Copyright © 2012 by Wendell Berry, from *New Collected Poems*. Reprinted by permission of Counterpoint.

"*Minobimaadizi*" by Kimberly Blaeser. Copyright © 2017 by Kimberly Blaeser. Reprinted by permission of the author.

"The Joins" by Chana Bloch from *Swimming in the Rain: New and Selected Poems, 1980-2015* (Autumn House Press, 2015). "The Joins" also appeared in the 2015 Pushcart Prize anthology and *Best American Poems 2015*. Reprinted by permission of the author.

"Surprised by Evening" from *Silence in the Snowy Fields*. Copyright © 1962 by Robert Bly. Published by Wesleyan University Press. Used by permission.

"Putting in a Window" by John Brantingham. Copyright © 2002 by John Brantingham. First published in *Byline Magazine*. Reprinted by permission of the author.

"Trough" and "Wooden Boats" by Judy Sorum Brown. Copyright © 2000 by Judy Sorum Brown. First published in *The Sea Accepts All Rivers & Other Poems* (Miles River Press, 2000). Reprinted by permission of the author.

"Flowering" by Linda Buckmaster. Copyright © 2017 by Linda Buckmaster aka Huntress Press. First published in *Heart Song & Other Legacies*. Reprinted by permission of the author.

"This Morning" from *Happy Life*. Copyright © 2011 by David Budbill. Reprinted with the permission of The Permissions Company, Inc., on behalf of Copper Canyon Press, www.coppercanyonpress.org.

"a song with no end" from *The Night Torn Mad with Footsteps* by Charles Bukowski. Copyright © 2001 by Linda Lee Bukowski. Reprinted by permission of HarperCollins Publishers.

"Learning from Trees" by Grace Butcher. First published in *Poetry* (April 1991). "On the Necessity of Snow Angels for the Well-Being of the World" by Grace Butcher. Copyright © 2016 by Grace Butcher. Reprinted by permission of the author.

"Blackbirds" by Julie Cadwallader Staub. First published in *The Mennonite*. "Longing" first published in *Dreamseeker Magazine*. "Midlife" first published by *The Writer's Almanac*. Reprinted by permission of the author. All three poems will appear in her new collection, *Wing Over Wing* (forthcoming from Paraclete Press, 2019).

"No More Same Old Silly Love Songs" by Neil Carpathios. Copyright © 2017 by Neil Carpathios. First published in *Beyond the Bones* (FutureCycle Press, 2009). Reprinted by permission of the author.

"Late Fragment." Excerpt from *A New Path to the Waterfall*, copyright © 1989 by the Estate of Raymond Carver. Used by permission of Grove/Atlantic, Inc. Any third-party use of this material, outside of this publication, is prohibited. From *All of Us* by Raymond Carver published by Harvill Press. Reprinted by permission of The Random House Group Limited.

"blessing the boats" from *The Collected Poems of Lucille Clifton*. Copyright © 1991 by Lucille Clifton. Reprinted with the permission of The Permissions Company, Inc., on behalf of BOA Editions Ltd., www.boaeditions.org.

"On How to Pick and Eat Poems" by Phyllis Cole-Dai. Copyright © 2016 by Phyllis Cole-Dai. Reprinted by permission of the author.

“Moon” from *Picnic, Lightning*, by Billy Collins. © 1998. Reprinted by permission of the University of Pittsburgh Press.

“In the Middle” by Barbara Crooker. Copyright © 2005 by Barbara Crooker. First published in *Yarrow* (1998) and then in *Radiance* (Word Press, 2005). “Sometimes I Am Startled Out of Myself” copyright © 2005 by Barbara Crooker. First published in *The Christian Century* (2003) and then in *Radiance* (Word Press, 2005). “Praise Song” copyright © 2005 by Barbara Crooker. First published in *Windhover* (2004) and then in *Radiance* (Word Press, 2005). Reprinted by permission of the author.

“Think of Others.” From *Almond Blossoms and Beyond*, published by Interlink Books, an imprint of Interlink Publishing Group, Inc. Text copyright © Mahmoud Darwish/Actes Sud, 2009; translation copyright © Mohammad Shaheen, 2009. Reprinted by permission. www.interlinkbooks.com

“In Early Evening” by Kirsten Dierking. Copyright © 2013 by Kirsten Dierking. First published in *Tether* (Spout Press, 2013). Reprinted by permission of the author.

“No Fishing” by David Allan Evans. First published in *Great River Review* and then in *Real and False Alarms* (BkMk Press, 1985). Reprinted by permission of the author.

“Winter Grace” by Patricia Fargnoli. Copyright © 2013 by Patricia Fargnoli. First published in *Poet Lore* and then in *Winter* (Hobblebush Books, 2013). Reprinted by permission of the author.

“The Cure for It All” by Julia Fehrenbacher. Copyright © 2017 by Julia Fehrenbacher. First published in *The Huffington Post* and then in *She Will Not Be Quiet* (e-book, 2017). Reprinted by permission of the author.

“The Offering” and “The Quiet Listeners” by Laura Foley. Copyright © 2007 by Star Meadow Press. First published in *Syringa* (Star Meadow Press, 2007). Reprinted by permission of the author.

“On Pain” by Kahlil Gibran from *The Prophet: A New Annotated Edition*. Copyright © 2012 Oneworld Publications. Used by permission.

“Winter Poem” from *My House* by Nikki Giovanni. Copyright © 1972 by Nikki Giovanni, renewed 2000 by Nikki Giovanni. Reprinted by permission of HarperCollins Publishers.

“Twilight” from *Poems 1962-2012* by Louise Glück. Copyright © 2012 by Louise Glück. Reprinted by permission of Carcanet Press Limited and Farrar, Straus and Giroux.

“Gracias/Grace” by Rafael Jesús González. Copyright © 2017 by Rafael Jesús González. First published in *The Montserrat Review*, No. 6, Spring 2003. Reprinted by permission of the author.

“Evening Star” by Charles Goodrich. Copyright © 2003 by Charles Goodrich. First published in *Insects of South Corvallis* (Cloudbank Books, 2003). Reprinted by permission of the author.

“When I Am Wise” by Mary Gray. Copyright © 2002 by Wildsong. First published in *Wilderness Magazine*. Reprinted by permission of the author.

"Now is the Time" from the Penguin publication *The Gift: Poems of Hafiz* by Daniel Ladinsky. Copyright © 1999 by Daniel Ladinsky and used with his permission. "Companion for Life" and "Parallel the Care the Dancer Takes" from the Penguin publication *A Year With Hafiz: Daily Contemplations*. Copyright © 2011 by Daniel Ladinsky and used with his permission.

"The Good News" by Thich Nhat Hanh. Reprinted from *The Engaged Buddhist Reader* (1996), edited by Arnold Kotler with permission of Parallax Press, Berkeley, California, www.parallax.org.

"Blue Herons" by Twyla M. Hansen. Copyright © 1997 by Twyla M. Hansen. First published in *Hurakan* and *Wellsprings: Six Nebraska Poets* (University of Nebraska-Kearney Press, 1995), then in *In Our Very Bones* (A Slow Tempo Press, 1997). "Fog" copyright © 2017 by Twyla M. Hansen. First published in *Panoply: A Literary Zine* and then in *Rock • Tree • Bird* (The Backwaters Press, 2017). Reprinted by permission of the author.

"For Calling the Spirit Back from Wandering the Earth in Its Human Feet," from *Conflict Resolution for Holy Beings: Poems* by Joy Harjo. Copyright © 2015 by Joy Harjo. Used by permission of W. W. Norton & Company, Inc.

"When I Taught Her How to Tie Her Shoes" by Penny Harter. Copyright © 2017 by Penny Harter. First published online by *Hospital Drive: The Literature and Humanities Journal of the University of Virginia School of Medicine*. Reprinted by permission of the author.

"Rankin Ridge" by Linda M. Hasselstrom. Copyright © 1993 by Linda M. Hasselstrom. First published in *Dakota Bones: The Collected Poems of Linda Hasselstrom* (Spoon River Poetry Press, 1993). Reprinted by permission of the author.

"Postscript" from *Opened Ground: Selected Poems 1966-1996* by Seamus Heaney. Copyright © 1998 by Seamus Heaney. Reprinted by permission of Faber and Faber Limited and Farrar, Straus and Giroux.

"Love for Other Things" from *Darkness Sticks to Everything: Collected and New Poems*. Copyright © 1993 by Tom Hennen. Reprinted with the permission of The Permissions Company, Inc., on behalf of Copper Canyon Press, www.coppercanyonpress.org.

"In Plowboy's Produce Market" by Donna Hilbert. Copyright © 2004 by Donna Hilbert. First published in *Traveler in Paradise: New and Selected Poems* (PEARL Editions, 2004). Reprinted by permission of the author.

"Wage Peace" by Judyth Hill. Copyright © 2002 by Judyth Hill. First published in M. Adams (Ed.), *Singing this great body back together: In remembrance of September 11* (Baculite Publishing, 2002). Reprinted by permission of the author.

"I Am Going to Start Living Like a Mystic" from *Lay Back the Darkness: Poems* by Edward Hirsch, copyright © 2003 by Edward Hirsch. Used by permission of Alfred A. Knopf, an imprint of the Knopf Doubleday Publishing Group, a division of Penguin Random House LLC. All rights reserved. Any third-party use of this material, outside of this publication, is prohibited. Interested parties must apply directly to Penguin Random House LLC for permission.

"Meeting the Light Completely" from *The October Palace* by Jane Hirshfield. Copyright © 1994 by Jane Hirshfield. Reprinted by permission of HarperCollins Publishers.

"The Word" by Tony Hoagland from *Sweet Ruin*. Copyright © 1993 by the Board of Regents of the University of Wisconsin System. Reprinted courtesy of The University of Wisconsin Press.

"Journey" from *Rounding the Human Corners*. Copyright © 2008 by Linda Hogan. Reprinted with the permission of The Permissions Company, Inc., on behalf of Coffee House Press, Minneapolis, Minnesota, www.coffeehousepress.org.

"the door" by Miroslav Holub from *Poems Before & After: Collected English Translations*, translated by Ian & Jarmila Milner et al. (Bloodaxe Books, 2006). Reproduced with permission of Bloodaxe Books.

"Instructions" by Sheri Hostetler. Copyright © 2017 by Sheri Hostetler. First published in *A Cappella: Mennonite Voices in Poetry*, edited by Ann Elizabeth Hostetler (University of Iowa Press, 2003). Reprinted by permission of the author.

"The Moment." Copyright © by Marie Howe. First published on Poets.org. https://www.poets.org/poetsorg/poem/moment-0 (accessed on March 25, 2017). Reprinted by permission of the author.

"The Cure" by Albert Huffstickler from *Walking Wounded*, Backyard Press 1989. Reprinted courtesy of The Southwestern Writers' Collection at Texas State University.

"At the Teahouse, 6am" and "Mind Wanting More" by Holly J. Hughes. Copyright © 2004 by Holly J. Hughes. First published in *America Zen: A Gathering of Poets* by Ray McNiece and Larry Smith (Harmony Series, Bottom Dog Press, 2004). Reprinted by permission of the author.

"There was a time I would reject those" by Muhyiddin Ibn al-'Arabi from *Leading from Within: Poetry That Sustains the Courage to Lead*, edited by Sam M. Intrator and Megan Scribner. Copyright © 2007 by the Center for Courage and Renewal. All rights reserved. Used by permission.

"Seas" by Juan Ramón Jiménez from *The Soul is Here for Its Own Joy*, edited and translated by Robert Bly. Copyright © 1995 by Robert Bly. Reprinted by permission of Georges Borchardt, Inc., for Robert Bly and by the heirs of Juan Ramón Jiménez.

"You Are There", from *Love Comes First: Poems* by Erica Jong, copyright © 2009 by Erica Mann Jong. Used by permission of Tarcher, an imprint of Penguin Publishing Group, a division of Penguin Random House LLC. Copyright © Erica Mann Jong, 2008, 2017. All rights reserved.

"Mimesis" from *Alight*. Copyright © 2013 by Fady Joudah. Reprinted with the permission of The Permissions Company, Inc. on behalf of Copper Canyon Press, www.coppercanyonpress.org.

Untitled ("The Guest is inside you") from *Kabir: Ecstatic Poems* by Robert Bly, copyright © 2004 by Robert Bly. Reprinted by permission of Beacon Press, Boston.

"Prayer for the Dead" from *Prayers & Run-on Sentences* by Stuart Kestenbaum. Copyright © 2007 by Stuart Kestenbaum. Reprinted by permission of the author.

"Saint Francis and the Sow" from *Mortal Acts, Mortal Words* by Galway Kinnell. Copyright © 1980 and renewed 2008 by Galway Kinnell. Reprinted by permission of Houghton Mifflin Harcourt Publishing Company. All rights reserved.

"Visiting Mountains" from *Sure Signs: New and Selected Poems*, by Ted Kooser, copyright © 1980. Reprinted by permission of the University of Pittsburgh Press.

"Stone" by Danusha Laméris. "Thinking" copyright © 2014 by Danusha Laméris. First published in *The Sun Magazine* and last published in *The Moons of August* (Autumn House Press, 2014). Reprinted by permission of the author.

"For the Sake of Strangers" from *What We Carry*. Copyright © 1994 by Dorianne Laux. Reprinted with the permission of The Permissions Company, Inc., on behalf of BOA Editions, Ltd., www.boaeditions.org.

"One Heart" from *Book of My Nights*. Copyright © 2001 by Li-Young Lee. Reprinted with the permission of The Permissions Company, Inc., on behalf of BOA Editions, Ltd., www.boaeditions.org.

"A Gift" from *Sands of the Well* by Denise Levertov, copyright © 1996 by Denise Levertov. Reprinted by permission of New Directions Publishing Corp. and Bloodaxe Books.

"The Second Music" by Annie Lighthart. Copyright © 2013 by Airlie Press. First published in *Iron String* (Airlie Press, 2013). Reprinted by permission of the author.

"What Else" by Carolyn Locke. Copyright © 2015 by Carolyn Locke. First published in *The Place We Become* (Maine Authors Publishing, 2015). Reprinted by permission of the author.

"Wakarusa Medicine Wheel" by Denise Low. Copyright © 2017 by Denise Low. Reprinted by permission of the author.

"Because even the word *obstacle* is an obstacle" by Alison Luterman. Copyright © 2010 by Alison Luterman. First published in *The Sun Magazine*. Reprinted by permission of the author.

"A Poem for My Daughter" and "The Mosquito Among the Raindrops" by Teddy Macker. Copyright © 2017 by Teddy Macker. First published in *This World* (White Cloud Press, 2015). Reprinted by permission of the author.

"Rain on Water" by Freya Manfred. Copyright © 2008 by Freya Manfred. First published in *Swimming With a Hundred Year Old Snapping Turtle* (Red Dragonfly Press, 2008). "The Owl Cries at Night" copyright © 2003 by Freya Manfred. First published in *My Only Home* (Red Dragonfly Press, 2003). Reprinted by permission of the author.

"A Momentary Creed" from *The Shadow of Sirius*. Copyright © 2008 by W. S. Merwin. Reprinted with the permission of The Permissions Company, Inc., on behalf of Copper Canyon Press, www.coppercanyonpress.org.

"On Pilgrimage" from *New and Collected Poems: 1931-2001* by Czeslaw Milosz, page 359. Copyright © 1988, 1991, 1995, 2001 by Czeslaw Milosz Royalties, Inc. Reprinted by permission of HarperCollins Publishers and Penguin Books Ltd.

"Bali Hai Calls Mama" by Marilyn Nelson. Copyright © 1997 by Louisiana State University Press. Reprinted by permission.

"Trees" from *The Collected Poems of Howard Nemerov*. Copyright © 1977 by Howard Nemerov. All rights reserved. Reprinted by permission of University of Chicago Press.

"Keeping quiet" ("A callarse") from *Extravagaria* by Pablo Neruda, translated by Alastair Reid. Published by Jonathan Cape. Copyright © 1958 Fundación Pablo Neruda. Translation copyright © 1974 by Alastair Reid. Reprinted by permission of Farrar, Straus and Giroux and The Random House Group Limited.

"Feather at Midday," reprinted from *Healing: A Woman's Journey from Doctor to Nun* (2010) by Sister Dang Nghiem with permission of Parallax Press, Berkeley, California, www.parallax.org.

"The Uncertainty Principle" from *Little Girls in Church*, by Kathleen Norris, copyright © 1995. Reprinted by permission of the University of Pittsburgh Press.

"Sifter" from *A Maze Me: Poems for Girls* by Naomi Shihab Nye. Copyright © 2005 by Naomi Shihab Nye. Reprinted by permission of HarperCollins Publishers.

"My Father at the Piano" by Mary O'Connor. Copyright © 2017 by Mary O'Connor. Reprinted by permission of the author.

"Fluent" from *Conomara Blues: Poems* by John O'Donohue. Copyright © 2001 by John O'Donohue. Published by Doubleday. Reprinted by permission of HarperCollins Publishers and The Random House Group Limited.

"When I Am Among the Trees," from the volume *Thirst* by Mary Oliver, published by Beacon Press, Boston. Copyright © 2006 by Mary Oliver. Used herewith by permission of the Charlotte Sheedy Literary Agency, Inc.

Untitled ("This is what was bequeathed us") from *How Beautiful the Beloved*. Copyright © 2009 by Gregory Orr. Reprinted with the permission of The Permissions Company, Inc., on behalf of Copper Canyon Press, www.coppercanyonpress.org.

"One's Ship Comes In" by Joe Paddock. Copyright © 2009 by Joe Paddock. First published in *Dark Dreaming, Global Dimming*, Red Dragonfly Press. Reprinted by permission of the author.

"Lie Down" by Nancy Paddock. Copyright © 2006 by Nancy Paddock. First published in *Trust the Wild Heart*, Red Dragonfly Press. Reprinted by permission of the author.

"Consider the Space Between Stars," from *Insomnia: Poems* by Linda Pastan. Copyright © 2015 by Linda Pastan. Used by permission of W. W. Norton & Company, Inc., and Linda Pastan in care of the Jean V. Naggar Literary Agency, Inc.

"Brotherhood" by Octavio Paz, translated by Eliot Weinberger, from *The Collected Poems 1957-1987*, copyright © 1986 by Octavio Paz and Eliot Weinberger. Reprinted by permission of New Directions Publishing Corp. "Brotherhood" ("Hermandad"), translated by Eliot Weinberger from *Octavio Paz: Collected Poems* by Octavio Paz. Copyright © 1987, 1988 by Octavio Paz and Eliot Weinberger. Reprinted with the permission of Pollinger Limited (www.pollingerltd.com) on behalf of the Estate of Octavio Paz.

"A Sacrament" by Paulann Petersen. Copyright © 2006 by Paulann Petersen. First published in *A Bride of Narrow Escape* (Cloudbank Books, 2006). Reprinted by permission of the author.

"To have without holding" from *The Moon Is Always Female* by Marge Piercy, copyright © 1980 by Middlemarsh, Inc. Used by permission of Alfred A. Knopf, an imprint of the Knopf Doubleday Publishing Group, a division of Penguin Random House LLC; and by permission of the Wallace Literary Agency. All rights reserved.

"Zazen on Ching-t'ing Mountain" by Li Po from *Crossing the Yellow River: Three Hundred Poems from the Chinese*, translated by Sam Hamill. Copyright © 2000 by Sam Hamill. Reprinted with the permission of The Permissions Company, Inc., on behalf of Tiger Bark Press, www.tigerbarkpress.com.

"Getting Up Early" from *Living Things* by Anne Porter. Copyright © 2006 by Anne Porter. Reprinted by permission of Steerforth Press.

"Take Love for Granted" by Jack Ridl. Copyright © 2013 by Wayne State University Press. First published in *Practicing to Walk Like a Heron* (Wayne State University Press, 2013). Reprinted by permission of the author.

"Ich liebe meines Wesens.../I love the dark hours of my being," from *Rilke's Book of Hours: Love Poems to God* by Rainer Maria Rilke, translated by Anita Barrows and Joanna Macy, translation copyright © 1996 by Anita Barrows and Joanna Macy. Used by permission of Riverhead, an imprint of Penguin Publishing Group, a division of Penguin Random House LLC.

"Entrance" by Rainer Maria Rilke, translated by Dana Gioia, from *99 Poems: New & Selected*. Copyright © 2016 by Dana Gioia. Reprinted with the permission of The Permissions Company, Inc. on behalf of Graywolf Press, Minneapolis, Minnesota, www.graywolfpress.org.

"We Are of a Tribe" by Alberto Ríos. Copyright © 2014 by Alberto Ríos. First published in *Goodbye, Mexico: Poems of Remembrance*, edited by Sarah Cortez (Texas Review Press, 2014). Reprinted by permission of the author.

"Then too there is this" by J. Allyn Rosser. Copyright © 2004 by J. Allyn Rosser. First published in *Poetry* and then in *Foiled Again* (New Criterion, 2007). Reprinted by permission of the author.

"A Little Stone in the Middle of the Road, in Florida" by Muriel Rukeyser, from *Out of Silence: Selected Poems*, edited by Kate Daniels. Copyright © 1992 by TriQuarterly Books. Used by permission. All rights reserved.

“A Community of the Spirit” by Rumi, translated by Coleman Barks. Copyright © 1995 by Coleman Barks. First published in *The Essential Rumi*. Reprinted by permission of the author.

“The Muse Is a Little Girl” by Marjorie Saiser. Copyright © 2001 by Marjorie Saiser. First published in *Lost in Seward County* (The Backwaters Press, 2001). Reprinted by permission of the author.

“Burning the Journals” by Robyn Sarah. Copyright © 1992 by Robyn Sarah. First published in *The Touchstone: Poems New & Selected* by Robyn Sarah (House of Anansi, 1992). “Solstice” copyright © 1998 by Robyn Sarah. First published in *Questions About The Stars* by Robyn Sarah (Brick Books, 1998). Reprinted by permission of the author.

“An Observation.” Copyright © 1966 by May Sarton, from *Collected Poems 1930-1993* by May Sarton. Used by permission of W. W. Norton & Company, Inc., and A. M. Heath & Co. Ltd.

“Sunday Afternoon” by Nancy Ann Schaefer. Copyright © 2015 by Nancy Ann Schaefer. First published in *The Conway* [New Hampshire] *Daily Sun*. Reprinted by permission of the author.

“Moth Koan” by Richard Schiffman. Copyright © 2013 by Richard Schiffman. First published in *Rattle*. “Smart Cookie” copyright © 2012 by Richard Schiffman. First published in *Rosebud Magazine*. Reprinted by permission of the author.

“Instructions for the Journey” by Pat Schneider. Copyright © 1999 by Pat Schneider. First published in *Olive Street Transfer* (Amherst Writers & Artists Press, 1999). “The Patience of Ordinary Things” copyright © 2003 by Pat Schneider. First published in *The Patience of Ordinary Things* (Amherst Writers & Artists Press, 2003). Reprinted by permission of the author.

“Versions of Ghalib: Ghazal I” by Ghalib, interpreted by Ruth Schwartz. Copyright © 2005 by Ruth L. Schwartz. First published in *Dear Good Naked Morning* (Autumn House Press, 2005). Reprinted by permission of the author.

“Walking a Field into Evening” by Larry Smith. Copyright © 2015 by Bottom Dog Press, Inc. First published in *Lake Winds: Poems* by Larry Smith (Bottom Dog Press, 2015). Reprinted by permission of the author.

“Afterwards” from *The Way It Is: New & Selected Poems*. Copyright © 1993, 1998 by William Stafford and the Estate of William Stafford. Reprinted with the permission of The Permissions Company, Inc. on behalf of Graywolf Press, Minneapolis, Minnesota, www.graywolfpress.org.

“Ancient Language” by Hannah Stephenson. Copyright © 2016 by Hannah Stephenson. Reprinted by permission of the author.

“Soundings” by Joyce Sutphen. Copyright 2004 by Joyce Sutphen. First published in *Naming the Stars* (Holy Cow Press, 2004). “The Last Things I’ll Remember” copyright © 2010 by Joyce Sutphen. First published in *First Words* (Red Dragonfly Press, 2010). Reprinted by permission of the author.

"Miracle Fair" from *Miracle Fair* by Wislawa Szymborska, translated by Joanna Trzeciak. Copyright © 2001 by Joanna Trzeciak. Used by permission of W. W. Norton & Company, Inc.

"The Bare Arms of Trees" by John Tagliabue from *New & Selected Poems: 1942-1997.* © National Poetry Foundation, 1998.

"The Bright Field" from *Laboratories of the Spirit* by R. S. Thomas. London. MacMillan 1975. Reproduced with permission of Pan Macmillan via PLSclear.

"A Brief Détente" by Rosemerry Wahtola Trommer. "Still Life at Dusk" copyright © 2012 by Turkey Buzzard Press. First published in *The Less I Hold* (Turkey Buzzard Press, 2012). "The Way It Is" first published on *AYearofBeingHere.com*. Reprinted by permission of the author.

"Earthworms" by Lynn Ungar. Copyright © 2012 by Lynn Ungar. First published in *Bread and Other Miracles* (AuthorHouse, 2012). "Camas Lilies" copyright © 1995 by Lynn Ungar. First published in *Blessing the Bread* (Skinner House Books, 1996). "The Way It Is" copyright © 2014 by Lynn Ungar. Reprinted by permission of the author.

"Lost" from *Traveling Light: Collected and New Poems*. Copyright 1999 by David Wagoner. Used with permission of the University of Illinois Press.

"Love After Love" from *The Poetry of Derek Walcott 1948-2013* by Derek Walcott, selected by Glyn Maxwell. Copyright © 2014 by Derek Walcott. Reprinted by permission of Farrar, Straus and Giroux and Faber and Faber Ltd.

"I Will Keep Broken Things" from the book *Hard Times Require Furious Dancing*. Copyright © 2010 by Alice Walker. Reprinted with permission of New World Library, Novato, CA. www.newworldlibrary.com

"Rutabaga" by Laura Grace Weldon. Copyright © 2011 by Laura Grace Weldon. First published in *Tending* (Aldrich Press, 2013). Reprinted by permission of the author.

"Lakol Wicoun" by Lydia Whirlwind Soldier. Copyright © 1999 by Lydia Whirlwind Soldier. First published in *Memory Songs* (Center for Western Studies, 1999). Reprinted by permission of the author.

"Sweet Darkness" by David Whyte from *The House of Belonging*, copyright © Many Rivers Press, Langley, WA USA. Printed with permission from Many Rivers Press, www.davidwhyte.com.

"Another Ocean" by Ruby R. Wilson. Copyright © 2015 by South Dakota Poetry Society. First published in *Four Quarters to a Section* (South Dakota State Poetry Society, 2015). Reprinted by permission of the author.

"Bedside Manners" by Christopher Wiseman. Copyright © 2005 by Christopher Wiseman. First published in *In John Updike's Room: Poems New and Selected* (The Porcupine's Quill).

About the Editors

Poetry of Presence (www.poetryofpresencebook.com) is Phyllis Cole-Dai's seventh book, and her only volume of poetry. She unites her passion for writing and music composition with a commitment to humanitarian service. All her creative work is driven by a profound desire to help create a more humane world for this and future generations. Originally from Ohio, she now makes her home in Brookings, South Dakota, with her husband and teenage son, the loves of her life. In 2013 the city of Brookings awarded her the 14th annual Dorothy and Eugene Butler Human Rights Award. Learn more at www.phylliscoledai.com.

Ruby R. Wilson (www.rubyrwilson.wordpress.com) graduated from South Dakota State University with majors in German and Geography. She had a hard time figuring out what she wanted to be when she grew up, but has now found her niche as an archivist in the South Dakota State University Archives & Special Collections Department, and as a freelance writer and photographer. She has published three poetry chapbooks: *Campus Sketches: Images of South Dakota State University in Word and Photograph*, *At the Rim of the Horizon* (Finishing Line Press), and *Maybe the Moon is Falling*, one of four winners of the 2014 South Dakota State Poetry Society chapbook competition. She lives on a small acreage in rural Brookings County with her husband Jim. She can sometimes be seen gathering seeds from big bluestem and other native plants, or gazing at stars that aren't crowded out by city lights.

Acknowledgments

Our creation of this anthology has been part spiritual exercise, part labor of love, and above all, a gesture of kinship. We offer a special word of appreciation to these people for their contributions:

We begin with Chuck Woodard, retired English professor and dear friend: You were the first person we ever heard remark that some poems are particularly "mindful." A direct line runs from that observation, made years ago, to this book. Thank you.

To the editors and poets who offered nuts-and-bolts advice on the process of anthologizing and marketing—Dick Allen, Barbara Crooker, Sheri Gilbert, Linda Hasselstrom, Andrea Hollander, Robyn Sarah, Megan Scribner, Larry Smith, Christine Stewart, and others we might have forgotten: It was just like you said. We were in for a crazy ride. But we benefitted greatly from your guidance and encouragement.

To the librarians and staff at the Brookings Public Library and the Hilton M. Briggs Library at South Dakota State University in Brookings, SD: Thank you for fulfilling our many Interlibrary Loan requests and advising us on permissions with such good humor and promptness.

To the photographer David Moynahan, whose beautiful image, "Great Egret Bow," graces the cover: Your eye and talent are surpassed only by your heart. We're grateful.

To Ginny Connors and her team at Grayson Books: You took a chance on this anthology when nobody else would. Thank you for loving the poetry enough, and trusting our instincts enough, to open the door. We're so happy we walked through it. The world needs more publishers like you.

To the poets: Without you this book wouldn't exist. We bow to your craft and your service, and to the big, wild horse of your muse. Hang on for the ride, fingers clutching the mane.

To our husbands and children: What can we say? You put up with our long hours and our hair-pulling. You made possible our writing retreats, offered sound (and sometimes absurd) advice, brewed coffee and poured libations, kept us well fed (red devil sauce, indeed!) and made sure we didn't take ourselves too seriously. ("Anybody for a wine summit?")

Finally, to our friendship, which carried us even when we didn't know where we were going. Ever forward, never straight.

Deep peace to all.

CPSIA information can be obtained
at www.ICGtesting.com
Printed in the USA
FFOW02n2027080917
39711FF